"This timely self-help workbook will be valuable for people stru[...]
anxious thoughts. It contains important information, a great deal c[...]
reports, exercises, worksheets, and troubleshooting techniques. It will benefit many readers and
provide a useful resource for professionals. I strongly recommend it."

—**S.J. Rachman**, emeritus professor at the Institute of Psychiatry, King's College London;
and at the University of British Columbia, Vancouver

"David A. Clark, an internationally renowned and respected researcher and clinician provides therapists and clients a state-of-the-art self-help guide to overcome unwanted distressing thoughts that may
catch therapists as well as clients. It helps the reader to develop a better understanding of anxious
thoughts regardless of the diagnosis, and then provides them an excellent guide for effective self-
coping skills based on scientifically proven procedures and principles. It aims to make one his or her
own therapist and reclaim their freedom from being prisoners of their intrusive thoughts. Trust this
workbook instead of trusting your self-defeating anxious and intrusive thoughts."

—**Mehmet Sungur**, professor of psychiatry at the University of Marmara, and president
of the International Association of Cognitive Psychotherapy

"At long last, we have a groundbreaking workbook compiled specifically for those grappling with distressing, unwanted, and intrusive thoughts. David A. Clark has produced a scholarly yet practical
self-help manual that takes the reader systematically through a series of highly practical skills drawn
from the latest research and evidence-based interventions. The book is well structured and is filled
with information, self-assessments, exercises, and skills development that are immensely useful and
easy to follow. It is a must-read for those inflicted with unwanted, intrusive thoughts, as well as clini-
cians attempting to haul patients from their obsessional quagmire."

—**Chee-Wing WONG, PsychD**, associate professor in the department of psychology at
the Chinese University of Hong Kong

"From a world-leading expert on intrusive thoughts, this book will guide you through a series of exercises that will help you to understand your anxious thoughts, and importantly it will help you to use
new strategies to better respond to them. The book is based in the latest cognitive and behavioral
science as it applies to anxiety and mental intrusions, and promises to be useful, whether you're a
mental health professional who helps people with anxiety-related problems, or someone who struggles
with unwanted intrusions yourself."

—**Adam S. Radomsky, PhD**, professor of psychology, and director of the Anxiety and
Obsessive-Compulsive Disorders Laboratory at Concordia University in Montreal,
Quebec, Canada

"This book provides a detailed account of the nature and causes of unwanted intrusive thoughts, images, memories, and feelings that produce fear, pain, and suffering.... This book provides effective tools for dealing with intrusive cognitions, and it explains how to practice these tools and why they are useful. At the same time, it provides examples of non-useful strategies and describes why they are not effective.... David A. Clark is a clinician and researcher with extensive experience and acknowledged prestige in the realm of emotional disorders. *The Anxious Thoughts Workbook* is the result of a perfect combination of clinical experience and excellence in research."

—**Amparo Belloch, PhD**, professor of psychopathology, and head of the Unit for Research and Treatment of Obsessions and Compulsions at the University of Valencia, Spain

"David A. Clark shares effective, step-by-step approaches for combatting upsetting intrusive thoughts that contribute to anxiety, depression, and related problems. The book is filled with rich examples, practical exercises, and evidence-based tools—making it easy to learn the strategies. For anyone who struggles with anxiety, depression, or other problems associated with unwanted mental intrusions, I highly recommend this book!"

—**Martin M. Antony, PhD**, professor of psychology at Ryerson University and coauthor of *The Shyness and Social Anxiety Workbook* and *The Anti-Anxiety Workbook*

"*The Anxious Thoughts Workbook* by David A. Clark is an excellent step-by-step guide to overcoming the feeling that you are trapped by unwanted intrusive thoughts. Based on the best research, Clark takes us on a journey into the troubled mind and leads us out to setting aside the thoughts that often limit our daily lives. Filled with helpful forms and powerful techniques, this book will give you the tools to free you from your anxiety. Highly recommended."

—**Robert L. Leahy PhD**, author of *The Jealousy Cure*

"If you have bothersome, repetitive, anxiety-producing thoughts, *The Anxious Thoughts Workbook* is the solution. David A. Clark offers a proven, systematic solution to easing the distress associated with intrusive and unwanted thoughts. *The Anxious Thoughts Workbook* is based on the most recent and sophisticated scientific understanding of how we think, and offers true hope and help. The book teaches practical strategies that can enable you to lessen the self-critical, catastrophic, and negative thoughts that you may currently have. Clark is one of the world's leading experts on the connection between how we think and how we feel. *The Anxious Thoughts Workbook* is for you if you want to feel less anxious and distressed, and want to feel a greater sense of confidence and joy."

—**Dennis Greenberger, PhD**, coauthor of *Mind Over Mood*

"I first became aware of David A. Clark's work on intrusive thoughts as a master's student back in 1989 through his own groundbreaking studies in the early eighties. This book brings together all the clinical experience, theoretical work, and research Clark has conducted during his career to understand and develop effective strategies for different types of upsetting intrusive thoughts.... A very welcome addition to the literature for those who suffer from unwanted intrusive thoughts."

—**Mark Freeston, PhD**, research director and doctorate in clinical psychology at Newcastle University, United Kingdom

THE
ANXIOUS
THOUGHTS
WORKBOOK

Skills to Overcome the Unwanted Intrusive Thoughts
that Drive Anxiety, Obsessions & Depression

DAVID A. CLARK, PhD

New Harbinger Publications, Inc.

Publisher's Note

This publication is designed to provide accurate and authoritative information in regard to the subject matter covered. It is sold with the understanding that the publisher is not engaged in rendering psychological, financial, legal, or other professional services. If expert assistance or counseling is needed, the services of a competent professional should be sought.

Distributed in Canada by Raincoast Books

Copyright © 2018 by David A. Clark
        New Harbinger Publications, Inc.
        5674 Shattuck Avenue
        Oakland, CA 94609
        www.newharbinger.com

Cover design by Amy Shoup

Acquired by Ryan Buresh

Edited by Brady Kahn

All Rights Reserved

Library of Congress Cataloging-in-Publication Data

Names: Clark, David A., 1954- author.
Title: The anxious thoughts workbook : skills to overcome the unwanted intrusive thoughts that drive anxiety, obsessions, and depression / David A. Clark, PhD.
Description: Oakland, CA : New Harbinger Publications, Inc., [2018] | Includes bibliographical references.
Identifiers: LCCN 2017044314| ISBN 9781626258426 (pbk. : alk. paper) | ISBN 9781626258433 (pdf e-book) | ISBN 9781626258440 (epub)
Subjects: LCSH: Intrusive thoughts. | Anxiety--Prevention. | Affective disorders.
Classification: LCC RC531 .C5349 2018 | DDC 616.85/22--dc23 LC record available at https://lccn.loc.gov/2017044314

20   19   18

10   9   8   7   6   5   4   3   2   1   First Printing

Contents

Foreword

Throughout my careful reading of this book, I kept having the same positive thought: *This is an excellent book*. I wasn't deliberately trying to have that thought; it just kept popping into my head. It was a positive *mental intrusion* that led to positive feelings.

Positive thoughts such as these are rarely a problem, but negative thoughts can be. In standard cognitive behavior therapy (CBT), individuals learn how to identify distressing thoughts in order to evaluate and, ultimately, modify their inaccurate thinking. But, as David A. Clark describes, this process of evaluation is not always helpful, especially when negative thoughts are highly repetitive and unwanted. Throughout this workbook, Dr. Clark describes a different process to address these *intrusive thoughts* more effectively as he illustrates them with interesting and enlightening case examples.

When some people experience intrusive thoughts, they are able to shift their attention to something else fairly easily. (These are the people for whom standard CBT works very well.) Others, however, run into trouble, especially if their mental intrusions have deep personal significance. Those suffering from these more severe mental intrusions usually develop strategies to help control their thinking, and the problem is that these coping behaviors usually end up doing the opposite. After repeated and unsuccessful attempts to control or suppress them, unintended intrusive thoughts can become toxic, making them a real problem that must be dealt with in the real world.

This unique workbook teaches you what to do when your unwanted mental intrusions are specifically associated with depression, anxiety, guilt, worry, frustration, or obsessive-compulsive disorder. The strategies are based on research from cognitive neuroscience and experimental social cognitive psychology. *The Anxious Thoughts Workbook* contains systematic, clearly explained self-help exercises, worksheets, and other clinical resources that will help you gain control over distressing mental intrusions. Most importantly, they will help prevent your distressing mental intrusions from becoming toxic, allowing you to regain control of your runaway mind.

You can use this workbook on your own or in conjunction with psychotherapy to help address the plague of distressing mental intrusions that you experience. However you choose to use it, though, learning the strategies in *The Anxious Thoughts Workbook* will help you regain control over not just your mind, but also your life.

—Judith Beck
President, Beck Institute for Cognitive Behavior Therapy
Clinical Professor of Psychology, University of
Pennsylvania School of Medicine

Introduction

Do you experience bouts of anxiety, depression, or other negative emotions that seem to come out of the blue or are more intense than you would expect? If so, this workbook was written for you. *The Anxious Thoughts Workbook* tackles the problem of unwanted intrusive thoughts and how you can use the new science of mental control to reduce negative feelings and promote positive emotion. Over half the thoughts, images, and memories that pop into your mind are unexpected, spontaneous mental intrusions (Christoff 2012). You don't willfully produce these thoughts, but they're instantly drawn into your awareness without effort. Daydreaming and mind wandering are two common examples of spontaneous thought, but all of us experience hundreds of distinct intrusive thoughts throughout the day. Often we are barely aware of these mental intruders. They may be silly, stupid, or irrelevant thoughts that we don't really notice. They are insignificant noise in our head, and we easily ignore their presence.

But not all mental intrusions are meaningless head noise. Sometimes an intrusive thought, image, or memory involves something that we find intensely negative or threatening. These upsetting intrusions grab our attention, interrupt our train of thought, and can be incredibly difficult to ignore (Clark and Rhyno 2005; Rachman 1981). We can develop a preoccupation with these negative intrusions, so they become an important cause of sadness, anxiety, guilt, fear, and frustration. In fact, negative intrusive thoughts are a significant problem for people struggling with clinical disorders like major depression, generalized anxiety, post-traumatic stress disorder (PTSD), obsessive-compulsive disorder (OCD), addictions, eating disorders, and the like. If intrusive thinking is a normal part of brain function, you might be wondering how this type of thinking becomes such a problem for many people.

Unwanted Thoughts and Emotional Distress

For a century, psychologists have assumed that the answer to emotional distress lies deep in the human mind or psyche. Older forms of psychotherapy based on Freudian theory considered unconscious conflicts the root of anxiety and depression. Even the newer treatments, like cognitive behavioral therapy (CBT), assume that core beliefs underlie psychological distress

(A. T. Beck 1967; J. S. Beck 2011). *The Anxious Thoughts Workbook* takes a different approach to emotional disturbance. Here the focus is on the first unwanted thoughts that burst into the mind and set in motion an uncontrollable cycle of increasing distress. The key to understanding the cause of emotional pain and suffering is found in our response to these initial thoughts.

This workbook focuses on unwanted mental intrusions and how we try to control them. The central idea is that personal distress occurs when we consider an intrusive thought a highly significant negative experience that must be controlled (Rachman 2003). That is, we become convinced that we must not dwell on a certain thought and so work hard trying to push the thought out of our mind. But these mental-control efforts often end in failure, which then causes a further increase in emotional distress and magnifies the personal significance of the intrusion. This sets up a vicious cycle of increasing distress and unrelenting thoughts that can feel like you're losing your mind.

In *The Anxious Thoughts Workbook*, you will learn how to reverse this vicious cycle by stripping distressing intrusive thoughts of their meaning and using effective mental-control strategies. Some of the interventions are based on well-researched psychological treatments like CBT (Greenberger and Padesky 2016), mindfulness (Teasdale, Williams, and Segal 2014), and acceptance and commitment therapy (ACT) (Hayes, Strosahl, and Wilson 2011). Other features are derived from research in cognitive neuroscience and the social-clinical psychology of directed mental control (Christoff 2012; Killingsworth and Gilbert 2010; Rachman 2003; Wegner 1994b). To better understand the mental-control perspective on personal distress, consider the following case illustration.

Meredith's Story: A Struggle for Emotional Control

Meredith's life was full; actually it was way too full! Her days flew by with the demands of a full-time job, raising two school-aged children, caring for aging parents, supporting a professional husband, and volunteering for charities. With such comfort, security, and purpose, Meredith realized she was living a life of privilege. But lately Meredith noticed increasing bouts of anxiety and despair that hit her suddenly and lasted for hours.

When Meredith first started having these mood shifts, she blamed it on the hassles and burdens of daily living. Certainly, her life was hectic, but deep down she knew something had changed in her inner being. Everything now seemed to bother her, and she had so little patience. She became more negative and self-critical. She was filled with self-doubt and was worried about the future. To Meredith and her family, it was clear she was experiencing some type of emotional crisis and needed to regain control over her emotions.

Meredith started becoming more focused on how she was thinking and feeling. When she had a negative thought like *I'll never get it all done*, or *This is not good enough*, she tried hard to push the thoughts from her mind. She reminded herself to think positively and reassured herself that everything would be fine. When worried, she angrily told herself to stop it. At the office, she tried to distract herself with a heavy workload. But the more she tried to take control of her thoughts and feelings, the worse she felt. The unwanted thoughts became more frequent and distressing. She tried even harder to control the intrusions, becoming convinced that if she didn't change her attitude, she was about to bring ruin on herself and her family. But after weeks of struggling with self-control, Meredith gave up in despair. Despite her best efforts, nothing was working. She was puzzled by her seeming helplessness and concluded that she needed professional help.

Meredith realized she needed better control over her negative thoughts and feelings if she hoped to turn her life around. After all, self-control is an important ingredient of success and life satisfaction (Mischel 2014). But the more Meredith tried to ignore the negative thinking and replace it with positive thoughts, the more she felt anxious and depressed.

There are several reasons why Meredith failed in her efforts at mental and emotional self-control. For one thing, she was overthinking the significance of her negative intrusive thoughts. When thoughts like *I'll never get it all done* or *I'm letting everyone down* popped into her mind, they reminded Meredith that her thoughts and feelings were out of control. She immediately started thinking about the negative implications: that her seemingly poor mental control would lead to dire consequences. She thought about how she was letting down her family and coworkers, but most of all, she thought about how disappointed she was in herself.

As well, Meredith was trying too hard to control her thoughts. The more these negative intrusions interrupted her flow of thought, the harder she tried to ignore them, to push them down. She became desperate to change her thinking, but the harder she tried, the worse it got. She could not just let the thoughts sit in her mind; she felt she had to do something to get rid of them.

Finally, as the intrusions became more frequent and disruptive, Meredith found herself relying more and more on ineffective control strategies, like trying to actively suppress the thoughts, distract herself with anything, or even yell at herself for having such "stupid thoughts." In the end nothing was working. Her distress intensified, and Meredith wondered if she needed to take an extended leave from work or even be hospitalized.

Like Meredith, you may be struggling to regain control over unwanted distressing thoughts and feelings. You realize better self-control is needed, but the harder you try, the more you feel upset and frustrated with your failed efforts. This workbook can help you regain control over distressing thoughts and feelings. As with Meredith, you may be overemphasizing the importance of certain unwanted intrusive thoughts. Many of the exercises in this workbook will teach you how to downgrade your interpretations of significance, let go of excessive control effort, identify ineffective mental control, and adopt more helpful mental-control strategies. Some of this work will be demanding and may even seem counterintuitive.

You may be wondering how you can change the importance of these distressing thoughts when they are causing such a problem in your life. It is difficult to change our approach to self-control, so the workbook takes a gradual, step-by-step learning perspective with lots of instruction on how to apply the new science of mental control to your negative emotion. To get the most out of the workbook, it's important to understand its organization and how to make the best use of the exercises and worksheets.

About This Workbook

There are numerous workbooks on how to overcome anxiety and depression, so you may be wondering what is unique about *The Anxious Thoughts Workbook*. There are some fundamental differences to this workbook.

- It is the only workbook that focuses specifically on the unwanted mental intrusions that trigger emotional distress.

- It clearly specifies which mental-control strategies are the least effective for intrusive thoughts and feelings.

- It presents effective mental-control strategies that are derived from research in cognitive neuroscience and social-clinical psychology.

- It offers practical self-help interventions relevant for a broad range of negative emotions.

- It provides strategies that enhance positive intrusive thoughts and boost momentary happiness.

The workbook consists of eight chapters, each focused on a different aspect of unwanted intrusive thoughts and feelings and their control. The chapters build on each other, so you'll find it most helpful to read them in the order presented. If one of the chapters is especially relevant, you will want to spend more time in that chapter. The first two chapters provide important background information on the nature of unwanted intrusive thoughts and mental self-control. Chapters 3 through 7 provide guidance and instruction on how to adopt more effective self-control skills over anxiety, depression, and obsessive states. These chapters are filled with exercises and worksheets, so you'll want to spend most of your time in this part of the workbook. The final chapter focuses on a different aspect of emotional self-control. In this chapter, you'll learn how to use mental control to boost positive intrusive thoughts, so you can experience more happiness in your daily life.

If your experience with this workbook turns out to be disappointing, the appendix can help you troubleshoot why your self-help work was less than satisfactory. The appendix also provides information about special types of intrusive thoughts and other psychological conditions, like anxiety disorders, major depression, and obsessive compulsive disorder (OCD), that usually require treatment by a mental health professional. If you are wondering if this workbook is appropriate for the type of distressing thoughts and feelings that you have, you should proceed immediately to the appendix, read the information, and do the self-evaluation exercises offered there to help you determine whether you should be seeking professional help.

Getting the Most from This Workbook

The Anxious Thoughts Workbook is a workbook designed to help you learn more effective self-control of distressing intrusive thoughts and feelings. You'll be introduced to a unique approach to mental self-control, but for these skills to be therapeutic, you'll need to make a commitment to change. You may be tempted to settle for just reading through this workbook. However, to get the most out of it, you'll need to double down and do the exercises. You'll probably find some interventions more helpful than others, so you'll want to spend more time with the helpful ones. As well, some skills are harder to learn than others, so you'll want to slow down and take your time with the related exercises. You'll want to make copies of some worksheets, so you can use them repeatedly. Other times, you'll write your responses right in the workbook, so you have a permanent record of your work. Alternatively, you can download copies of the worksheets and exercises at the website for this book: http://www.newharbinger .com/38426. This is a great way to get extra copies of the worksheets in case you need more worksheet space to do the exercises.

The workbook focuses mainly on depression, anxiety, and obsessive thinking. Consequently, most of the case illustrations and examples involve these emotional states, although some references are made to frustration, guilt, and anger. Of course, the last chapter deals entirely with positive emotions like joy, contentment, and satisfaction. The case illustrations are clinical composites drawn on thirty-five years as a clinical psychologist treating individuals with emotional disorders, and so specific details of each case and their experiences with the workbook exercises are hypothetical presentations used to illustrate practical application of clinical skills.

Your decision to begin reading this workbook is an important step toward better emotional health. Your investment in this workbook demonstrates an openness to change: recognition that you need a different approach to managing negative emotion. A willingness to try something different and a determination to work on self-improvement are important ingredients in making meaningful change. So you are to be congratulated for exposing yourself to new possibilities of change. But it's important to keep your expectations realistic and to have patience. Don't expect big changes immediately. It will take time and repeated practice to change your mental-control strategies. Here's what to expect:

Change requires systematic work. Real change requires that you use the new mental-control strategies in your daily life.

Change requires insight. First you need to discover your problematic mental intrusions, how you interpret or understand them, and how you try to control them. Thus you'll need to do some self-assessment work initially, so you can benefit from the control skills discussed in later chapters.

Everyone is different. The intrusive thoughts that bother you most and how you respond to them will be unique to you. You may need to adapt the exercises to match your needs and situation.

Practice, practice, practice. To gain real benefit from this new approach to mental self-control, you need to practice the strategies over and over. Trying something new once or twice rarely makes a difference. You'll need to practice your new skills again and again until they feel more natural.

Be patient and exercise self-compassion. The old saying "Rome wasn't built in a day" is a good motto for this workbook. Your struggle with troubling thoughts and feelings may have persisted for many years. Transforming your mind takes time. Progress may be gradual. It is important to be kind and to adopt a compassionate, nonjudgmental attitude toward yourself (Baer 2014). After all, you are taking responsibility for your health and doing your best to deal with the distress in your life. Before turning to chapter 1, here once more is what you can expect to learn from *The Anxious Thoughts Workbook*:

- To identify the negative intrusive thoughts, images, or memories that drive your anxiety, depression, and other negative emotions.

- To determine your tolerance for unwanted mental intrusions and limited controllability.

- To develop a personal understanding of the mental processes involved in the persistence of distressing thoughts and feelings.

- To dial down the personal significance and threat attributed to problematic mental intrusions.

- To relinquish ineffective mental-control strategies and adopt more effective responses to your distressing intrusions.

- To feel more confident in your mental self-control and less concerned about losing control.

- To maximize positive thought and emotion and to reduce the effects of negative emotional states.

To determine whether you are meeting these learning objectives, you may want to return to this list from time to time as you proceed through this workbook. If you have not made the progress you would like against anxiety, depression, obsessions, or other distressing conditions, make sure to read the appendix and consider whether a mental health consultation might be beneficial. From this workbook, you'll gain fresh insights and learn more powerful self-control strategies that can bring renewed strength and balance to your emotional well-being. So it's time to get started on your journey of self-improvement. It begins with a better understanding of mental intrusions.

CHAPTER 1

The Unsettled Mind

Think back to the last time you were bored. Maybe you were stuck in traffic, mindlessly watching a TV program, or trapped in a tedious meeting at work. Can you remember what you were thinking? Probably not, but it's very likely you were daydreaming or your mind was wandering from one thought to the next. When bored, we are especially prone to intrusive thinking. Our mind switches into an automatic mode which generates free-floating thoughts that are entirely disconnected from each other and may have little relevance to our current situation. It's like our mind is always in an active, unsettled state, even when we feel understimulated. Of course, there are other times when our free-floating, or intrusive, thoughts take on a darker, more negative tone because they're triggered by a stressful or problematic situation. Our memory for this type of thinking is sharper because these thoughts focus on issues more important to our general well-being.

This chapter delves into the nature of unwanted mental intrusions and their role in personal distress. From this discussion, you'll gain a deeper understanding of your anxiety, depression, or obsessionality, and why you may be susceptible to mental intrusions. You'll also discover that intrusive thinking can be either a blessing or a curse in your quality of life. You'll learn about the origins of spontaneous thought and how it is necessary for normal brain function. The chapter is full of self-assessment checklists and other exercises intended to bring clarity to complex emotional states. You'll want to work your way slowly through this chapter, giving yourself time to fully absorb all of the self-assessment material. This will give you a solid foundation for applying the new science of mental control to your anxiety and depression. A good place to start is with an example of one of the most obvious forms of emotionally disturbing intrusive thoughts: obsessive doubt.

Daniel's Story: Dealing with Doubt

Doubt is a natural form of human thought, but for Daniel, doubt had become extreme and unreasonable. Practically any action or decision could trigger a relentless cycle of doubt. When leaving the house, Daniel doubted whether the water taps were completely off, if all the lights were switched off, or if the door was securely locked. When doubt popped into his mind, Daniel imagined all sorts of catastrophes caused by potential carelessness or mistakes. A water tap not completely turned off could cause the house to flood; a door not securely locked could invite intruders. Although Daniel realized his *what ifs* were highly unlikely and often absurd, his doubting intrusions made him so anxious that he'd compulsively check over and over to make sure everything was safe and secure. He fought valiantly against the doubt and the urge to check, but nothing helped. The checking was never totally convincing, however, and the more he did it, the more intense the anxiety and doubt. Eventually, Daniel came to realize that his doubt was a form of obsessive-compulsive disorder (OCD) and that he needed professional help.

Like Daniel, your distressing intrusive thoughts may have taken on an obsessive quality. If you are unsure, you can use the following checklist to determine the obsessiveness of your mental intrusions. This checklist contains some of the key characteristics of the obsessive thinking style. You can visit http://www.newharbinger.com/38426 to download other copies of this obsessive-thinking checklist to use with other distressing thoughts.

EXERCISE: Obsessive-Thinking Checklist

In the space provided, record your repetitive distressing thought, image or memory:

_____

_____

Next, place a checkmark (√) beside the statements that describe your experience with this thought, image, or memory. If a statement is irrelevant, leave it blank.

_____ 1. *The same thought, image, or memory pops into my mind over and over again.*

_____ 2. *It is very difficult to get the intrusive thought out of my mind.*

_____ 3. *When I have the intrusive thought, it makes me feel more upset or distressed.*

_____ 4. *I really don't want to have the intrusive thought.*

_____ 5. *I've developed certain compulsive rituals to deal with the intrusive thought, like washing, checking, redoing, rereading, or reordering.*

_____ 6. *I realize the intrusive thought is excessive or even absurd.*

_____ 7. *I can't ignore the intrusion; it completely captures my attention.*

If you checked off several of the statements, especially numbers 1, 2, and 5, your intrusive thinking may have obsessional characteristics. The interventions presented in this workbook are effective for obsessive thinking. However, because obsessions are a particularly difficult form of intrusive thinking, you'll need extra time with the various mental-control exercises found in this workbook. If you are seeing a mental health therapist, you should mention your findings from this exercise. If you're reading this workbook on your own and you suspect you might have OCD, consider contacting a mental health expert.

Daniel suffered intense levels of anxiety, and each time he could trace its origin to an obsessive doubt. However, not all emotional distress can be attributed to a single type of mental intrusion. Anxiety, depression, guilt, frustration, and other negative emotions are often triggered by a variety of unwanted intrusive thoughts, images, or memories. As a result, you may need a more extensive assessment to discover the type and intensity of emotional distress you experience with your unwanted mental intrusions. This chapter provides some assessment tools to help you better understand your anxiety, depression, and associated distressing intrusions.

What's Your Distress?

If you were drawn to *The Anxious Thoughts Workbook* because of anxiety or depression, you need to know that you're not alone in your struggles. Every year, 40 million (18.1 percent of) American adults experience a clinical anxiety disorder and 16.4 million adults (6.7 percent) have a diagnosable episode of major depression (Kessler et al. 2005). Together, anxiety and depression are responsible for a substantial amount of personal suffering and lost productivity for one in five Americans. Depression is characterized by persistent feelings of sadness or despair, loss of interest or pleasure, fatigue, low self-worth, and diminished motivation (American Psychiatric Association 2013). Anxiety disorders vary from a sudden surge in anxiety, called a *panic attack*, to a general feeling of unease or apprehension. Worry is often a prominent feature of more generalized anxiety. In some cases, anxiety or fear can be highly specific, such as feeling anxious only in social situations because you fear that others will evaluate you negatively. If you suspect you may have an anxiety or depressive disorder, consult the appendix for further guidance and recommendations for seeking treatment.

Even mild forms of anxiety or depression can significantly reduce life satisfaction (Fava and Mangelli 2001). Whether your symptoms are mild or intense, the mental-control strategies in this workbook can be helpful. The following exercise will help you assess your symptom severity.

EXERCISE: Checklist of Depressive and Anxious Symptoms

This checklist presents several prominent symptoms of depressed and anxious moods. Think back to how you've been feeling over the last two weeks, and place a checkmark (√) next to the descriptions in each column that are relevant to your emotional experience.

Depressed Mood	Anxious Mood
_____ *Frequently have episodes that last at least one hour of feeling sad, blue, down, empty, or discouraged*	_____ *Experience frequent episodes that last more than several minutes of feeling uneasy, apprehensive, or uncomfortable*
_____ *Generally feel a loss of interest or enjoyment in daily activities*	_____ *Often think about threat, harm, or danger happening to myself or significant others*
_____ *Often feel tired or have loss of energy for no apparent reason*	_____ *Often feel tense, physically aroused, or queasy when apprehensive*
_____ *Often think that my future looks bleak, hopeless, or meaningless*	_____ *Will avoid situations that cause a feeling of apprehension or threat*
_____ *Don't feel engaged in meaningful or fulfilling life goals*	_____ *Am highly concerned about maintaining a sense of safety or comfort*
_____ *Struggle with low self-esteem or lack of self-confidence*	_____ *Tend to think of the worst-case scenario*
_____ *Tend to focus on loss or failure in life experiences*	_____ *Consider myself to be a worrier*

_____	Tend to be pessimistic and highly self-critical	_____	Feel excessively uncomfortable or stressed when being evaluated
_____	Rarely experience happiness, joy, or contentment	_____	Often feel anxious when unexpected physical symptoms are experienced
_____	Consider myself a procrastinator	_____	Often must work at calming myself down
_____	Frequently lack motivation	_____	Consider myself a nervous, anxious person

Looking over the checklist, which symptoms seemed more relevant to you, those describing anxious mood or those describing depressed mood? Did you check off many of these symptoms or only a few? The more symptoms you checked off in a particular column, the more intense your emotional experience.

As you do the exercises in this workbook, you'll want to return to this checklist to evaluate your progress on symptom improvement. For now, this checklist can help you determine your pace ahead. The more symptoms you checked off, the more time and practice you'll need with various workbook exercises.

Distressing Thoughts and Feelings

Emotional distress includes many different types of unwanted thoughts and feelings that extend beyond the core symptoms of anxiety and depression. For example, Daniel struggled daily with intense anxiety because of his obsessive intrusions of doubt, but he also experienced other negative emotions like guilt and frustration over his failed self-control. Guilt was an important emotion that drove his fear of making mistakes, and he often felt frustrated by his inability to stop checking. These other unwanted thoughts and feelings were _complementary states_ of emotional distress.

Take a few minutes to complete the checklist in the next exercise to determine whether you experience any complementary states of emotional distress. This checklist includes a definition and clinical example of each mental and emotional state. Unwanted mental intrusions and diminished mental control feature prominently in each.

EXERCISE: Checklist of Distressing Mental and Emotional States

Consider each of the symptoms below and place a checkmark (√) next to the ones that you often experience when feeling upset or distressed. If you experience a symptom only occasionally or it does not cause much distress, then leave it blank.

Symptom State	Definition	Example
_____ Obsessions	Unwanted, unacceptable, and often irrational recurring intrusive thoughts, images, or urges that feel uncontrollable and distressing even though you try not to give in to the thought	Fearful of becoming contaminated from objects touched by others
_____ Worry	A process of negative, uncontrollable, and highly distressing mental problem solving intended to reduce the uncertainty of one or more imagined future negative or threatening outcomes for yourself or significant others	Thinking about your finances and whether you are saving enough for retirement
_____ Rumination	A passive form of repetitive, uncontrolled negative thinking in which you revisit the same concerns about the causes and consequences of your depression or some past stressful experience	Thinking *Why do I keep feeling so depressed? I have no right to feel so down. I don't know what I'll do if I can't pull out of this funk.*
_____ Excessive doubt	Highly focused attention on an imagined possibility of having committed an error or act of omission that could have unintended negative consequences for yourself or others	Driving to work and suddenly questioning whether you actually unplugged your hair straightener

_____	Jealousy	Distressing and uncontrollable cyclical mental preoccupation with your personal disadvantage or deprivation and its unfairness in comparison to one or more others	Incessantly thinking about how unfair it is that your coworker got the promotion and you're still stuck in a boring lower-paying position
_____	Guilt	Recurring thoughts, images, or memories of a past mistake, failure, or carelessness that is associated with significant regret, shame, or embarrassment	Accidentally spilling coffee on a friend's new sofa and not telling her
_____	Frustration	A sudden realization that a valued goal or course of action is being thwarted by circumstances beyond your personal control	Being stuck in traffic and realizing you'll be late for an important appointment

Did you find many of the symptoms in this checklist relevant to your emotional distress? And after all, who doesn't have occasional worry or ruminate on some past disappointment? But if worry, rumination, guilt, or any other symptoms feature prominently in your distress, it's important that you focus on these experiences when you practice this workbook's interventions. Again, you'll want to return to this checklist later in the book to review the troubling thoughts and feelings you targeted in your self-help work.

By completing the previous exercises, you have gained a deeper understanding of your emotional distress. As Sir Francis Bacon said, "Knowledge is power." Your work on these exercises represents a small act of self-empowerment.

Now it's time to turn to unwanted intrusive thoughts and to consider how they contribute to depression, anxiety, and obsessional states.

Hunting for Intrusions

Any thought, image, or memory can be an unwanted mental intrusion. The unwanted intrusive thoughts associated with anxiety and depression are characterized by

- spontaneous occurrence in the mind; that is, without effort or intention

- high unacceptability

- an ability to get your attention

- a capacity to interrupt concentration

- their upsetting or distressing quality

- being difficult to ignore, suppress, or dismiss

Whether a thought is an unwanted intrusion depends on your evaluation of the thought. In fact, the actual thoughts we find unwanted and intrusive can be unique to each of us. Daniel, for example, had numerous unwanted intrusive thoughts, but they all dealt with the same theme: *What if I forgot to do something?* Or *What if I accidentally caused harm or injury to someone?*

So my mental intrusions will be quite different from yours, but everyone experiences unwanted negative intrusive thoughts, images, or memories. Of course, the frequency and distressing quality of unwanted intrusions differs greatly from person to person. The first task, then, is to discover the mental intrusions at the heart of your own emotional distress and whether they are linked together by a common theme.

Becoming more aware of intrusive thinking is challenging because these thoughts often pop into the mind unexpectedly and then disappear before we know it. However, the intrusions most relevant to personal distress are tightly connected to our emotions, and if you're aware of how you feel, you can work back from the emotion to discover the intrusive thought that made you feel bad in the first place. There is also considerable research showing that certain types of thoughts are associated with specific mood states (Clark, A. T. Beck, and Alford 1999). This relationship is reciprocal, so certain thoughts trigger certain feelings and vice versa. Figure 1.1 illustrates this thought-feeling connection.

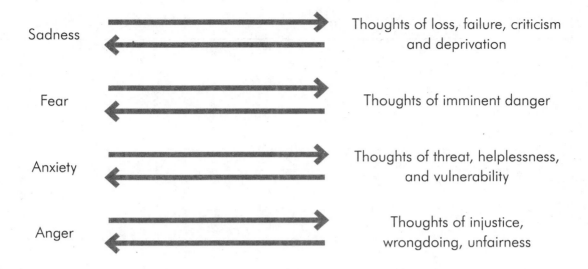

Figure 1.1. The Thought-Feeling Connection

Now it's time to discover the thought-feeling connections that occur when you're distressed.

EXERCISE: Thought-Feeling Record

Over the next two weeks, use this thought-feeling record to keep track of your experiences of negative thoughts and feelings. Note that thoughts can sometimes take the form of images or memories associated with your experiences of anxiety, depression, or other negative emotions. When you notice yourself having negative thoughts and feelings, briefly note the distressing situation or circumstance, and then list the associated negative feelings. Use the third column to record what you were thinking while feeling distressed, and then circle the first thought that went through your mind. You can visit http://www.newharbinger.com/38426 to download copies of this thought-feeling record.

Situation	Feeling	Negative Thinking
1.		
2.		
3.		
4.		

Developing a keen awareness of what you're thinking when feeling depressed or anxious is a fundamental skill taught in cognitive behavioral therapy (CBT) (Greenberger and Padesky 2016). When upset, it's more natural to be completely focused on the emotion, and it may seem unnatural to ask yourself, *Okay, I'm feeling depressed right now, so what am I thinking?* But focusing on your negative thoughts provides the answer for overcoming emotional distress. Of course, the mental-control approach goes one step further. It asks you to identify the first negative thought that intruded into your mind and started your negative feeling. So in the exercise, you not only identified your negative thoughts but also circled the thought that you believed first came into your mind.

Daniel was very aware of his doubting intrusive thoughts, so he didn't have to do a thought-feeling record to know what they were. However, he also experienced sudden periods of feeling blue or sad, which seemed to come completely out of nowhere, so he completed a thought-feeling record to discover the thought-feeling connection. After writing down several experiences of feeling sad, he noticed they often occurred after he got stuck in obsessional checking. His negative thinking went like this:

My OCD is getting worse.

I'll never get better.

It's hopeless.

I'm going to eventually get fired because I'm too slow.

I'm such a weak person.

I have no self-control.

As he captured more and more experiences of dysphoria, Daniel realized that the thought *I have no self-control* was the initial unwanted intrusive thought that led to feeling depressed. This was an important clue, which he used in building a mental-control intervention for his OCD.

Did you have difficulty identifying what you were thinking when feeling upset? Were you able to circle the first intrusive thought in the chain of thinking that led to anxiety or depression? If you are struggling with this exercise, give yourself time to practice identifying your intrusive thoughts before proceeding further with this chapter.

I've provided CBT to hundreds of clients, and practically everyone finds keeping a thought-feeling record difficult at first. So don't give up if you're struggling with this exercise. With practice and patience, you can learn to become more aware of your negative thinking. And like so many others, you'll find that heightened awareness of your thinking can have a therapeutic effect on your negative emotions. Increased cognitive self-awareness is an important part of greater self-control over unwanted thoughts and feelings. So I encourage you to keep using this thought-feeling record as you continue with the workbook.

Mental Intrusions: An Aspect of Creativity

Cognitive neuroscientists tell us that around 50 percent of our thinking is spontaneous, stimulus-independent thought such as daydreaming, mind-wandering, unwanted mental intrusions, and the like (Christoff 2012). This type of thinking is so common that it's actually been called the brain's default mode of operation (Killingsworth and Gilbert 2010). The brain centers responsible for spontaneous thought originate in the medial prefrontal cortex, posterior cingulate/precuneus region, and the temporoparietal junction of the brain, with extensive neural connections to other brain regions involved in self-control and emotion regulation (Dixon, Fox, and Christoff 2014). Spontaneous intrusive thinking, then, is not only normal but also essential to how the human brain operates.

If you've been struggling with distressing intrusive thoughts, you might be wondering if there's something wrong with you. Nothing could be further from the truth. Intrusive thinking, or what scientists call *undirected* thought, is important for human survival. Having frequent positive intrusive thoughts, for example, predicts resilience, growth, and life satisfaction (Baars 2010). Spontaneous positive thinking also contributes to creativity, which is critical for language, music, art, and the like (Wiggins and Bhattacharya 2014). So, being an intrusive thinker is not a negative characteristic but rather a very positive and enriching mental process. The goal is not to stop intrusive thoughts, if that were even possible, but rather to *harness your intrusions*, that is, to learn how to dampen down the effects of unwanted distressing intrusions and boost the benefits of positive or inspirational spontaneous thought.

Is it possible you've been so focused on negative thoughts and feelings that you've failed to recognize the benefits of your positive spontaneous thoughts? Maybe intrusive thinking is playing a more adaptive role in your life than you realize. For example, how often has a solution to a problem suddenly come to you out of the blue? At times, you might actually call it "inspiration." This happens often as a writer. I might be struggling with a particular passage, wondering how I can best convey a certain idea. Suddenly, out of nowhere, a solution to my writing impasse pops into mind. Sometimes it's a really good solution, and other times it's not such a good idea, but the point is, the sudden appearance of an unintended thought—call it inspiration or a positive intrusive thought—is important to the process. Our ability to think creatively, to generate solutions to problems, or to come up with a good idea is dependent on the part of our brain that engages in spontaneous unintended thought. So, if you are an intrusive thinker, congratulations! You have an amazing mental ability, but your challenge is to manage it wisely.

By now you might be asking yourself, *Am I an intrusive thinker?* Maybe you've been feeling so anxious or depressed that you've been overlooking the creative side of your intrusive thinking. Time to take a break from the negative chatter in your mind and use the following exercise to shift your attention to the possible positive, even creative, mental intrusions you may be experiencing more often than you realize. How often do ideas suddenly come to you that provide an answer to some work task? Or how often do you suddenly realize how you should respond to an interpersonal problem in your family? How often is intrusive thinking enriching your life, enabling you to deal with life's problems and challenges?

EXERCISE: Your Creative-Intrusions Diary

Over the next week or two, use this worksheet to record experiences in which a positive, creative, or inspirational idea spontaneously and unexpectedly pops into your mind. In the left-hand column, write down the situation, circumstance, or problem that you or someone you knew was facing. In the right-hand column, write down the sudden, unexpected thought or idea that enabled you to successfully deal with it. If you need more space to write, you can visit http://www.newharbinger.com/38426 to download a copy of this creative-intrusions worksheet.

Creative Intrusions Worksheet

Situation, Circumstance, or Problem	Creative Problem-Solving Intrusive Thought
1.	
2.	
3.	
4.	
5.	
6.	
7.	

Were you able to capture any positive or inspirational intrusions over the past week or two? Are you surprised at how often intrusive thinking actually helped you deal with a problem, circumstance, or difficult situation?

Daniel always considered his intrusive thinking to be problematic. But at work he often came up with important contrarian views at policy planning meetings. He seemed to have an intuitive ability to discover possible unintended consequences to the group's decisions. These contrarian views often came to him quite suddenly, seemingly out of the blue, with ease and conviction.

Like Daniel, you may be experiencing a dark, unintended side to your mental intrusions but realize you also have this positive, adaptive side to your creative mind. There is considerable similarity between positive intrusive thoughts and negative intrusive thoughts (Edwards and Dickerson 1987). Therefore, it's quite possible to frequently experience both. As you continue with this workbook, keep your creativity in mind, and remind yourself that your unwanted negative intrusive thoughts may be a product of your creative and imaginative mind. The final chapter focuses on boosting positive intrusions to promote happiness. In the meantime, this workbook will focus on controlling unwanted distressing thoughts.

The Ubiquity of Negative Intrusions

Unwanted and unpleasant mental intrusions are a fact of life for most people. You may be surprised to learn that even fairly disturbing intrusive thoughts, some of which you might consider to be disgusting, immoral, or repugnant, are reported by the average person. For example, a study of hundreds of university students from thirteen countries found that over 80 percent reported at least one unwanted, mildly distressing intrusive thought over a three-month period about contamination, doubt, harm or aggression, immoral sexual or religious concerns, or being a victim of violence (Radomsky et al. 2014). It is now a well-established finding that practically everyone has unwanted and distressing mental intrusions (Clark and Rhyno 2005). What differs among us is the frequency of our negative intrusions, the degree to which we can control them, and the intensity of our distress.

You may have assumed you're alone in your struggle with unwanted and distressing thoughts and feelings. If you find it hard to believe that others experience the same type of negative thinking, take some time to do the following negative-intrusions survey. Select five or six close friends, family members, or your spouse or partner, and ask them about their unwanted thoughts, images, or memories.

EXERCISE: Take a Negative-Intrusions Survey

Introduce this survey by asking the participant, "Do you ever have negative or upsetting thoughts, images, or memories that suddenly pop into your mind for no reason? You don't want to have this thought, image, or memory, you find it upsetting, and you would like to stop thinking about it, but it's hard to get your mind off it. It may pop into your mind quite randomly, and it may take you by surprise." Ask the person to describe these negative intrusions, and then use this worksheet to record the responses.

Name of Survey Participant	Negative Intrusive Thoughts, Images, or Memories
1.	
2.	
3.	
4.	
5.	
6.	

Did any of the survey participants deny having unwanted and distressing mental intrusions? If so, ask them if they'd be willing to track their thoughts over the next couple of days to determine if they experience more negative intrusions than they may have realized. Sometimes people initially deny having negative thoughts, because they tend to quickly forget about them. The thoughts aren't important, so they pay little attention to them. After intentionally tracking their intrusive thinking, however, they may be surprised to discover a significant amount of mental negativity.

As you'll learn from this workbook, the existence of negative intrusive thoughts and feelings is not the issue: what matters is how you deal with it. Again, some people seem to be more aware of their intrusive thoughts than others. This final section looks at whether some of us are more likely to experience distressing mental intrusions than others.

Are You an Intrusive Thinker?

There are many reasons why some people have more frequent and distressing intrusive thoughts than others. First, our life experiences can affect intrusive thinking. Stressful or traumatic life experiences can cause us to have repeated unwanted intrusive memories of the trauma for months or even years after the event. Second, our mood state affects the type of unwanted thoughts that intrude into our mind. If you're in a sad or depressed mood, you'll have more frequent negative intrusions of loss and failure; if anxious, your unwanted intrusions will focus on threat and danger; and if angry, you'll have more spontaneous thoughts about injustice and unfairness. Third, our personality affects whether we have few or many negative mental intrusions. People who are more emotional, more aware of their thoughts, and have greater difficulty controlling unwanted thinking will experience more frequent and distressing mental intrusions (Barahmand 2009; Munoz et al. 2013).

If people differ in their tendency to experience negative intrusive thoughts, you might be wondering about your risk level for this type of thinking. The following exercise can be used to estimate your natural propensity for intrusive thinking.

EXERCISE: Your Intrusion Proneness Checklist

Place a checkmark (√) beside the statements that describe your experience with intrusive thinking.

_____ *I'm a creative, divergent thinker.*

_____ *I have experienced a past traumatic event.*

_____ *I've had several major life problems or concerns.*

_____ *I experience frequent negative mood states.*

_____ *I consider myself an emotional person.*

_____ *I often overanalyze or overthink issues.*

_____ *I have difficulty controlling unwanted thoughts.*

If you checked three or more statements, you might be more inclined to experience frequent and distressing unwanted intrusive thoughts. However, this does not mean you are destined to live a life of perpetual distress, because there is probably a positive, creative side to your thinking that is being neglected.

If you're prone to negative-thought intrusions, it's important to be patient with your progress through the workbook and to keep your goals realistic. You may need to spend longer on certain exercises and cope with a higher level of negative intrusive activity than someone with a lower risk factor. But wherever you lie on the intrusion spectrum, you can expect to make progress in how you deal with unwanted anxious, depressive, and obsessive thinking.

Wrap-Up

Like millions of people, you may be struggling with negative emotional states like anxiety, depression, guilt, obsessions, anger, and the like. You may have started reading this workbook because you experience intense and persistent personal distress. Alternatively, your negative emotions may tend to be milder and more sporadic. Regardless of where you lie on the personal-distress scale, the key to better mental health starts with your unsettled mind. How we think affects how we feel, so changing your thoughts can bring healing and wholeness to your troubled emotions. In this chapter, you learned that

- Distressing mental intrusions are unintended thoughts, images, or memories that pop into our mind that are highly unacceptable, rich in negative emotion, and difficult to control.

- If your intrusive thinking is obsessive, you'll need more time practicing this workbook's intervention strategies.

- A better understanding of the symptoms associated with your distress is critical for designing a self-help treatment that works for you.

- Keeping a thought-feeling record is a useful tool for discovering the negative intrusions that trigger feelings of anxiety, depression, guilt, and other unpleasant emotions.

- Our ability to think spontaneously is a fundamental characteristic of brain function and necessary for our survival.

- Being an intrusive thinker may be linked to creativity; positive intrusive thoughts are associated with higher life satisfaction and well-being.

- The vast majority of people have negative intrusive thoughts. Whether you find your negative intrusions distressing or not depends on how you manage this unwanted form of thought.

In this chapter, you've seen that anxiety, depression, and other distressing emotional states are fueled by the presence of negative intrusive thoughts, images, and memories. Being aware of your intrusions and their connection to distress is an important part of the mental-control approach to distress. But unwanted negative intrusions are only part of the story. The second major theme of the workbook is mental control. We depend on mental self-control almost continuously throughout our wakeful hours, but what do you really know about mental control? How does it work and what are its limits? What happens when we begin to question our capacity for self-control? Chapter 2 will examine these and other issues.

Clinging to Self-Control

Have you ever wondered if you're losing your mind? Maybe you said something that you later regretted, or you behaved poorly and later felt really embarrassed, but when it happened, you just couldn't stop yourself. Or you've been having these strange, upsetting thoughts that suddenly pop into your mind, and you can't stop dwelling on them. These are examples of failed attempts at self-control, and we've all had many such experiences more often than we like. But why is it so hard to direct our thoughts, feelings, and behavior in ways that are right and good for us and others? Why does it seem easier to take a more distressing, sometimes even self-destructive, path? These are the kind of questions tackled by self-control researchers, which is the topic of this chapter.

As you've seen, the mind is an unsettled place, with hundreds of thoughts, images, and memories spontaneously appearing and disappearing without apparent direction or intent on our part. And yet, it's obvious we can direct our thoughts, choosing to concentrate our mental faculties on specific tasks, problems, or situations. If we had no mental control, we'd be unable to communicate with each other or interact with our external world. So how much control do we have over our thoughts and feelings? Psychologists have been researching this question for decades, and you'll be surprised at their findings. It turns out mental self-control may be more limited than you think.

This chapter explores various aspects of self-control and how you can begin to understand the strengths and weaknesses of your own thought controllability. It begins with what it means to have self-control, or willpower. Often when people are depressed or anxious, they blame themselves, believing they lack the willpower to get better, but willpower actually tends to fluctuate, so it's important to know what can strengthen or weaken it. This chapter then delves into the subject of mental self-control, which is the ability to choose which thoughts to concentrate on and which to ignore. You'll learn what influences our level of mental control, and you'll confront one of the great paradoxes of the human mind: the harder we try to not think about something, the more we're drawn to do the exact opposite, which is to think about it. It's like the thought grows in strength the more you try to resist it. You'll also explore how the fear of losing control contributes to anxiousness about your mental state. In addition to providing background information, this chapter offers some self-exploratory exercises to lay the foundation for learning more effective ways to promote self-control.

Emma's Story: Trapped in a World of Despair

Emma had been battling depression for months. Known for her high energy, enthusiasm, and productivity, Emma experienced her first depression after breaking off her engagement. The heartbreak she experienced was so profound, it seemed to affect every area of her life. Day after day, she felt dejected, sullen, and numb. She lost all interest in work and social activities. She felt unrelenting fatigue, spending most evenings in bed, binge-watching movies. Emma knew she was only making the depression worse by her withdrawal and inactivity. But she couldn't seem to muster the willpower to change. Her mind was flooded with negativity like *I don't want to do anything* and *I'm just too exhausted*. These became Emma's unwanted intrusive thoughts. She wanted to get back to her old self, but she couldn't seem to get beyond the intrusions. Once the *I can't* or *I won't* thoughts took hold, she couldn't shake them. She was convinced she had no willpower, that she had become a helpless victim of her own negative thoughts and feelings.

Emma was filled with self-blame for being stuck in depression. Her therapist gave her lots of good advice, suggesting she increase her social contact, go to the gym, and set realistic daily goals, but Emma couldn't seem to follow through. She berated herself for having no willpower and even questioned whether she had enough strength to face the ordinary demands of life. Emma felt lost in a land of despair with no will to leave.

How Willpower Works

When we can't force ourselves to do something, we often blame it on weak willpower. Psychologists use various terms for willpower, such as self-control or self-regulation. Willpower is the ability to override natural and automatic tendencies in the pursuit of some valued, long-term goal. This often involves relinquishing short-term attractions and following society's norms and rules (Bauer and Baumeister 2011).

Willpower is essential for life as we know it. It's a basic process involved in common mental functions like decision making, reasoning, and intelligent thought. Take a daily experience like getting to work. This simple act requires enormous willpower. You must force yourself to leave a warm, comfortable bed against your natural desire to fall back to sleep. You then venture into a cold, dark house, go through the same self-care routine that you do every morning, eat the same boring breakfast, and then battle crowded highways and streets to arrive at a highly stressful job. You do all this to purchase the desired amenities of life, satisfying the long-term goals of comfort and security for yourself and your loved ones. This is only one simple example of how you exert self-control in your daily life. Multiply this by the dozens of times throughout the day that you choose a harder path in pursuit of prized goals and values. Clearly, willpower is critical to your very survival.

This ability to exert self-control is rooted in a neural system called *executive function*, which can be found in the prefrontal cortex (PFC), a part of the brain also critical for goal attainment and emotion regulation (Wagner and Heatherton 2011). Willpower is possible because of PFC activation, which enables us to inhibit unwanted thoughts, feelings, and behavior that would distract us from pursuing our life goals and desires. The PFC also enables us to maintain our focus on thoughts, emotions, and actions that advance our goals.

Willpower, of course, has its limits, and it varies in strength from one moment to the next (Mischel 2014; Vohs and Baumeister 2011). Sometimes we feel strong and able to resist our immediate impulses, whereas other times we immediately cave in. Many factors can influence the strength of our willpower. No doubt you can easily recall times when your self-control was weak. It may take greater effort to remember times when you exerted strong self-control.

You can use the next exercise to record times when you demonstrated good self-control. It could be something important, like forcing yourself to work on a project you'd been procrastinating on, or it could be accomplishing a more routine but boring task, like doing the laundry, tidying up the house, or washing the car. If you have difficulty coming up with an example of exerting willpower, take note of your activities over the coming week and select an occasion when you forced yourself to do something to achieve a desired goal. Emma, for example, always made sure she ate healthy food, even when she was feeling depressed and unmotivated to eat.

EXERCISE: When Did You Exert Strong Willpower?

Write down a desired goal you forced yourself to work on even when you had little motivation to do it.

_____

_____

_____

Were you able to identify an example of exerting strong willpower? Can you come up with more than one example? Before working on other areas where you may have less self-control, it is important to recognize how often you have an adequate amount of willpower to get things done in your life.

It's not like you always take the easiest route and never make progress on important life goals. Emma, for example, noted that she had strong self-control over her diet because she felt passionate about good dietary habits, and she knew she could continue to eat healthily because she'd been doing it for years. More importantly, when Emma thought about her willpower over food, she felt encouraged that she could make progress on other issues if only she used a more effective self-control strategy.

Now that you've had a chance to reflect on your times of high self-control, it's important to consider other occasions when you've struggled with willpower. Working on low self-control is especially important because avoidance, procrastination, and goal abandonment are common features of anxiety, depression, and other negative emotional states.

You can use the next exercise to record a personal goal—something you'd like to start doing or stop doing—which you lack motivation or willpower to achieve. It could be an important task at home or at work or a trivial activity that you can't get yourself to do. Emma knew she would probably feel a little better if she went out with her friends, but she couldn't force herself to contact even her closest friend. Night after night, she procrastinated making the call, choosing instead to stay at home alone.

EXERCISE: When Have You Felt Your Willpower Was Weak?

Write down a desired goal that you've been unable to achieve because you can't overcome low motivation.

_____

_____

_____

Was coming up with an example of weak willpower easier than coming up with an example of strong willpower? If so, don't be discouraged. If you are having difficulty exerting self-control, it's not because there's some flaw in your character. You've just been reminded that you can exhibit strong willpower with various activities in your daily life.

It's important to recognize that having low self-control is not something fixed or unchangeable. Low self-control is actually a problem of motivation strategy, which is something you can work on.

Looking at Your Motivation Strategies

Certain strategies that we use when we hope to achieve a goal actually diminish our willpower even though we may not be aware of it at the time. Have you considered that you might be relying on ineffective strategies to motivate yourself?

EXERCISE: Weak Willpower-Strategies Checklist

Choose a time when weak willpower was particularly relevant to your personal distress. Next, read through the following statements and place a checkmark (√) beside the statements that help to explain your lack of willpower at the time.

_____ 1. *I was spread too thin; trying to exercise self-control over too many different things at once.*

_____ 2. *I was not pursuing a valued or well-defined goal.*

_____ 3. *I was focused on a goal that would not produce much improvement in my current situation.*

_____ 4. *I never really believed I could attain the goal.*

_____ 5. *I was trying to motivate myself while in a negative mood state.*

_____ 6. *I tried to make a change on my own with little support from others.*

_____ 7. *I often engaged in self-criticism while trying to reach the goal.*

_____ 8. *I chose to work on the goal when physically exhausted.*

_____ 9. *I have neglected physical exercise, so I have less energy.*

_____ 10. *I became quite emotional and overly self-absorbed when trying to motivate myself.*

_____ 11. *I tried to motivate myself by focusing on distant or remote benefits of self-control.*

_____ 12. *If possible, I choose to avoid self-control opportunities as much as possible.*

Did you check off one or more statements? If so, do you have a better sense of why you've struggled with low motivation to achieve your goal? Each statement reflects a strategy that diminishes self-control. When you have strong willpower, you're using more effective motivation strategies, but when self-control is weak, you resort to easier but less effective motivation strategies (refer to the checklist items you endorsed).

Emma, for example, knew she needed to increase social contact with her friends. But she ended up using ineffective strategies to deal with her low motivation. For example, she didn't really believe that more social activities would improve her mood state (number 2), she was convinced she just wasn't a friendly person (number 4), she'd put off thinking about calling her friend until after work when she was tired and most depressed (numbers 5 and 8), and she berated herself for being such a terrible procrastinator (number 7). When it came to motivating herself to be more sociable, Emma undermined her motivation by adopting weak willpower strategies.

Emma decided to come up with a motivation action plan to achieve her goal of increasing her social contact with friends. To come up with some strong motivation strategies, Emma stated the opposite of numbers 2, 4, 5, 7, and 8. She intentionally worked on

determining whether she did feel better after social interaction, thereby changing her belief in the importance of being more sociable.

realizing she was capable of being friendly by taking note of times when she acted friendly to others.

deciding that she would text her friend (about meeting for lunch) earlier in the morning when she felt more rested and was in a slightly better mood state.

countering her self-criticalness by reminding herself that she was working on self-improvement and making some progress, but that it would take time and she needed patience.

Now that you have a better understanding of your willpower and your motivation strategies, it's time to put this knowledge to work with a new motivation action plan to achieve your goal. For additional copies of the Motivation Action Plan, visit http://www.newharbinger .com/38426.

EXERCISE: Motivation Action Plan

Write down a goal that you've been unable to achieve because of low willpower (you can name the goal you described earlier in this chapter).

_____

How have you been trying to achieve the desired goal?

_____

_____

What do you think you need to do to reach the desired goal?

_____

_____

Review your responses to the weak willpower-strategies checklist, and revise your previous ineffective motivation strategies to come up with a new list of strong motivation strategies (hint: do the opposite of what you've been doing). As a guideline, you may want to review how Emma did this. Write down your new strategies.

1. _____

2. _____

3. _____

4. _____

5. _____

Once you've created your motivation action plan, it's time to put it into practice. You might want to keep the action plan handy, so you can refer to it whenever you're reminded of the desired goal.

Emma loaded her motivation plan on her smartphone as a to-do list, so she could frequently check the list throughout the day. This way she could remind herself to stop and take a minute to text her friends about meeting up after work or about their plans for the weekend.

Motivating yourself to break the habit of avoidance and procrastination takes effort and determination. But if you're patient with yourself and take small steps, using effective motivation strategies, you can make the changes that will help reduce unwanted thoughts and feelings.

Of course, the willpower strategies we've been discussing are broadly relevant to all forms of thought, behavior, and emotion. It's important to remember that willpower is strengthened with the use of motivation strategies that emphasize the pursuit of high-valued goals in a rational, reasoned, and confident manner. So work on improving your motivational strategies is an important pathway to better emotional health and well-being.

The next section focuses in on mental self-control, which is especially useful for the unwanted intrusive thoughts that contribute to your emotional distress.

The Mental-Control Paradox

Mental control refers to a conscious, directed effort to shift attention away from unwanted thoughts, images, memories, sensations, feelings, or urges and toward wanted mental events that will create a desired state of mind (Wegner and Pennebaker 1993). For example, at this moment, you are using mental control to read and understand this passage. You're actively trying to concentrate on the workbook and inhibit intrusive thoughts that might interrupt your concentration, such as thinking about what you'll have for lunch, something you heard on the news, or an argument you had with your spouse last night.

To maintain attention and concentration, mental control must achieve two aims: to maintain attention on wanted thoughts and to selectively inhibit irrelevant, unwanted, and distracting thoughts. Effective mental control, then, is a balancing act between attending to what we want to think about and inhibiting or suppressing the irrelevant or unwanted distracting intrusions. Of course, we're not perfect in executing this mental balancing act. Sometimes we seem to have good mental control, and then other times we can't seem to concentrate, no matter how hard we try. During those times when mental self-control seems to be slipping, you may try even harder to focus on the wanted thoughts and suppress what you don't want to think. But how successful are you? No doubt you've stumbled into one of the great mysteries of the mind, which can be called the *mental-control paradox*.

Most things we want to learn to do in life benefit from practice. For example, the more you may practice at music, dance, sport, or any other skill, the better you will get at it. And generally, the more we practice and the harder we work at something, the greater the chance of our achieving important life goals. Well, unfortunately, this is not the case when it comes to efforts at mental control. There is considerable scientific evidence that the harder we try to control our unwanted thoughts, the worse they get. It's called an ironic mental process (Wegner 1994a). If you don't believe me, try the white-bear experiment. It consists of two parts: thought retention and thought dismissal. For this experiment, you'll need a notepad and pencil along with a smartphone or other timer.

EXERCISE: White-Bear Experiment: Part 1. Thought Retention

Find a quiet place in your house where you can sit comfortably without interruption. Now close your eyes, take a couple of slow deep breaths, and relax. After a minute or two of relaxation, read the following thought-retention instructions. Then set your timer for two minutes and follow the instructions.

Thought-retention instructions: Close your eyes and force yourself to think about a white bear. *You should try as hard as you can to keep your mind focused on a white bear.* If other thoughts intrude into your mind so that you lose the white-bear thought, simply note the interruption with a tally mark on a blank sheet of paper, and then gently return your attention to the white bear. After the two-minute interval, stop the experiment, open your eyes, and count up the number of interruptions you experienced while trying to think about a white bear.

If you're like most people, you probably couldn't think about the white bear continuously for even two minutes. No doubt you experienced several unwanted intrusive thoughts that broke your concentration and caused you to lose focus multiple times. Notice that even though you were putting great effort into mental control, you still couldn't maintain perfect attention on a very simple idea for even two minutes.

The takeaway message from this exercise is twofold:

1. Mental control is far from perfect, even with great effort.

2. Concentration and attention are fluid, constantly shifting from one thought to the next.

Now it's time to do the second part of the white-bear experiment where you try to eliminate a thought, which is called *thought dismissal*. Again you'll need a notepad and pencil along with your smartphone or other timer.

EXERCISE: White-Bear Experiment: Part 2. Thought Dismissal

Again start by closing your eyes, taking a couple of slow deep breaths, and relaxing. After a minute or two, proceed with the dismissal part of the experiment after reading the following instructions.

Thought-dismissal instructions: Reset your timer or watch for two minutes, close your eyes, and for the next two minutes, try not to think about a white bear. *You should try as hard as you can to suppress or prevent any thought of a white bear from entering your mind.* If the thought of a white bear intrudes into your mind, make a tally mark on the sheet of paper, and then gently turn your attention to other thoughts.

After completing this second phase of the experiment, look at the number of times the white-bear thought intruded into your mind over the two-minute interval. If you're like most people, you probably found it even harder to suppress the white-bear thought (thought dismissal) than to intentionally think about a white bear (thought retention).

With thought dismissal, the white bear became an unwanted intrusive thought. Did you find that the harder you tried not to think about a white bear, the more the bear came into your mind? If this was your experience, then you've experienced the paradox of mental control (see figure 2.1). That is, the harder you try to suppress an unwanted thought, the more it will intrude into your mind.

 Greater Mental Effort = Poorer Mental Control

Figure 2.1. The Mental-Control Paradox

Over the last couple of decades, hundreds of psychological experiments have shown that active attempts to directly inhibit or suppress unwanted thoughts are ineffective, at best, and probably make the experience of negative distressing thoughts worse (Rassin 2005; Wegner 1994a). The research indicates that trying to suppress unwanted thoughts sometimes causes an immediate increase in their frequency, whereas at other times it causes a resurgence of the intrusion after the efforts to suppress the thoughts cease. Also, a number of factors can make the negative effects of thought suppression worse; these include being in a negative mood state, placing undue importance on the unwanted thought, or tending to rely on thought suppression to deal with unwanted thoughts and feelings. The bottom line is that trying too hard to not think about an unwanted, distressing thought is most often futile and even counterproductive. Excessive mental control effort often amplifies the intensity and persistence of negative emotional states. This is why reducing mental-control effort is a major emphasis in this workbook.

Emma had several intrusive thoughts relevant to her depression. One of the most frequent was *Poor me, I'm so unhappy and depressed*. She interpreted this thought as a sign of self-pity, and so it made her feel guilty. She tried to suppress this thought by replacing it with more positive thinking or by criticizing herself for being so self-centered. But these strategies didn't help, and the harder she tried to suppress her thoughts of how unhappy and depressed she was, the worse they got. Emma was living out the paradox of mental control.

As you will see, the antidote to the mental-control paradox is learning to let go, to take a more accepting approach to the unwanted thought. You can think of your distressing intrusive thoughts like a net that entangles your mind. The harder you struggle against the thought, the more trapped you become in your mental torment. And as with being caught in a net, the best strategy for unwanted intrusions is to stop struggling.

When it comes to mental control, how we perceive our ability to control our thoughts plays an important role in how we feel. Given the counterintuitive nature of mental control and its capacity to fuel intense personal distress, is it any wonder that some people develop a fear of losing control?

Fear of Losing Control

This chapter opened with the question "Have you ever wondered if you're losing your mind?" Experiencing unwanted and distressing thoughts, images, memories, or feelings, day in and day out, can make you begin to lose confidence in your mental faculties. As you experience failures in self-control, you may begin to worry that your loss of control could get worse. You might wonder, *What if I completely lose control, so I can no longer function or, worse, my mind snaps and I cause harm to myself or my loved ones?* In the extreme, this fear of losing control can cause us to doubt our sanity. The question might be *Could I actually go insane and become incapable of looking after myself or my family?*

Fear of losing control is a common element in fear and anxiety, especially panic disorder. Fear of losing control can directly increase feelings of anxiety and personal vulnerability. It can also cause you to try even harder to control unwanted intrusive thoughts and feelings, because you're afraid that further erosion of control could lead to a complete mental breakdown. So the adverse effects of the mental-control paradox could be even greater for people who are fearful of losing control. Fear of losing control can also intensify feelings of uncertainty. Difficulty tolerating uncertainty is a major issue in anxiety disorders, so anything that causes more uncertainty will increase anxious feelings.

We each differ in the importance we place on mental self-control. If you're not so concerned about control of your thoughts and feelings, you may be tolerant of a wandering mind and even unwanted intrusive thoughts. If you place a high value on controlling your thoughts and feelings, then you may tend to feel anxious about your failure to control unwanted mental intrusions. You may even worry at times about your sanity because of unwanted and unusual thoughts that frequently pop into your mind. As you can see, the more importance you place on mental self-control, the greater the likelihood you'll feel anxious when mental control fails, like what happened in the white-bear experiment.

How comfortable are you with limited control over unwanted thoughts and feelings? Are you able to let unwanted negative thoughts wander through your mind, or do you feel like you're in a battle to regain control over a renegade mind? Are you afraid of losing control, especially mental self-control? The next exercise will help you gauge your level of tolerance for unwanted spontaneous thought.

EXERCISE: Your Tolerance of Mental Uncontrollability

Below you'll find five statements that deal with key features of thought controllability. Place a checkmark (√) beside the statements that apply to you.

_____ I am often upset by recurring negative thoughts, images, or memories that feel uncontrollable.

_____ I wonder if my mind could snap or if I lack a normal amount of mental self-control.

_____ I believe my problem is lack of willpower or self-control.

_____ I feel anxious when I can't stop myself from thinking certain unwanted thoughts.

_____ When I lose control of my thoughts, I'm concerned that I might eventually act on them.

If you checked several statements, then it's likely you'll find it difficult to accept limited mental control over your unwanted thoughts and feelings. You may be at greater risk for fear of losing control. Maybe you're feeling entangled in that mental net mentioned earlier. If so, you are taking the first step toward freedom from this struggle. Knowledge and insight is the first step in learning how to work with the paradox of mental control rather than against it.

Of course, there's much more to learn that will help you regain confidence in your mental health. But just knowing that greater mental effort can be counterproductive is an important insight that can change how you deal with your anxiety, depression, or obsessionality.

Wrap-Up

"The harder I try, the worse it gets." If this is your sentiment, it's likely you're feeling discouraged with your efforts to regain control of your life and eliminate the long shadow of anxiety, depression, or obsessive thinking. No doubt, you've been thinking that you lack willpower and that if you tried harder to discipline your mind, your distress would disappear and life would be so much better. But as you now understand, willpower can be erratic, and the paradox of mental control makes no exceptions. Here are some takeaway thoughts from this chapter:

- Self-control, or willpower, involves the pursuit of long-term valued goals by overriding natural tendencies to settle for immediate comfort and ease.

- Willpower is strengthened with the use of motivation strategies that emphasize the pursuit of high-valued goals in a rational, reasoned, and confident manner.

- Developing an action plan to overcome procrastination or pursue neglected life goals can improve your emotional state.

- Mental control is a paradoxical process in which the harder you try to suppress unwanted intrusive thoughts, the more problematic they become, and excessive mental-control efforts often amplify emotional distress.

- Improving tolerance for unwanted spontaneous thought and accepting the limits of mental self-control are the primary treatment objectives of this workbook.

Don't be discouraged. What you've been learning about intrusive thinking and the limits of mental control can actually help you overcome anxiety, depression and obsessive thinking. The chapters you've just read have provided you with the knowledge you need to use the interventions that follow. It's time to begin working on the thoughts and feelings that give rise to your emotional disturbance, which is the subject of the next chapter.

CHAPTER 3

Control Skills: Self-Discovery

In the days before GPS and Google Maps, I remember getting hopelessly lost! This often happened when foolishly trying to navigate an unfamiliar city without a decent map in hand. At first, I felt annoyed by my carelessness, but the longer I was lost, the more anxious I got. On a couple of occasions, I spent over an hour trying to get my bearings. When that happened, anxiety gave way to fear, confusion, and an intense feeling of helplessness. Do you recall the last time you were really lost? I'm sure you'll agree it's a terrible experience. But the momentary anxiety associated with being lost doesn't compare to the anguish felt when bewildered by unwanted distressing thoughts and feelings that persist despite our best efforts at self-control.

If you're feeling a little lost and discouraged by your emotional state, it's important to first figure out what's wrong and then develop a plan that guides you toward emotional wholeness and well-being. In the first two chapters, you learned about unwanted intrusive thoughts and the limits of mental control, but you might be wondering, *How can this new knowledge help lessen my feelings of anxiety, depression, or obsessiveness?* To use the new science of mental control, you'll need a better understanding of the mental processes that drive your emotional condition. You'll need an individualized plan, a mental road map, to give you some direction on how to overcome these distressing thoughts and feelings.

Meaningful change begins with greater self-understanding. This chapter will present a mental-control model to help you discover the unwanted mental intrusions that trigger your negative emotions, search for maladaptive mental-control efforts, and assess whether the significance or importance you give to the intrusion is problematic. You'll then combine all of this information to formulate your own mental-control profile, which will be your road map for applying new interventions to your emotional distress. But first, the story of a young woman named Samantha will help to illustrate how all of this works.

Samantha's Story: Crippled by Social Anxiety

Samantha, a twenty-one-year-old university student, had always been shy and nervous around others, especially people she didn't know. Interacting with peers was especially anxiety provoking. Despite efforts to overcome her self-conscious, nervous manner around others, the anxiety would eventually become so overwhelming that she'd end up leaving early or avoiding social activities altogether. Samantha experienced many anxious thoughts that all focused on a fear of negative evaluation by others. Most often the anxiety began with the intrusive thought *You're going to feel anxious and uncomfortable.* That thought alone was enough to set in motion a cycle of anxiety and worry about spending time with others. Sometimes Samantha pictured people laughing about her afterward and even mocking the way she talked. On other occasions, she'd remember the time a guy had spoken to her and, out of sheer terror, she'd said something ridiculous in response. Despite her attempts to suppress these anxious mental intrusions and to convince herself that she'd be okay, the thoughts persisted, and with them came an overwhelming sense of anxiety. Avoidance became the only viable option. Samantha was convinced her future looked bleak, dominated by loneliness, despair, and alienation from others.

The Mental-Control Model

Usually we treat spontaneous thinking as unimportant mental noise that we can easily ignore. However, if you are anxious, depressed, or emotionally upset, certain types of unwanted thoughts can become a focal point of your attention. If you then misinterpret the intrusion as a highly significant threat to your emotional health, you may try to directly control or suppress the unwanted thought. This effort often fails, which stimulates other forms of pathological thinking such as worry, rumination, obsessions, and the like, and you become caught in a vicious cycle of escalating negative thought and feeling.

This vicious cycle of distress is apparent in Samantha's experience of social anxiety. When reminded of an upcoming social activity, Samantha has the intrusive thought *I can't do this. I'll be so anxious. It will be unbearable.* She becomes immediately aware of the intrusion because it's a personally significant thought. She's convinced it's a highly accurate prediction of how she'll feel, because this is what has happened in the past. Samantha can feel herself getting anxious, just thinking about her social anxiety. So she then tries to suppress the thought. She tells herself it'll be okay; maybe she won't feel so anxious this time. But she doesn't believe it. She tries to distract herself but can't shake the thought. Finally, she reacts with annoyance and anger, telling herself to stop being so stupid. By now, though, she's into full-blown anxiety, with unhealthy worry about how she'll manage the dreaded event.

Figure 3.1 outlines the key components of the mental-control model of emotional distress.

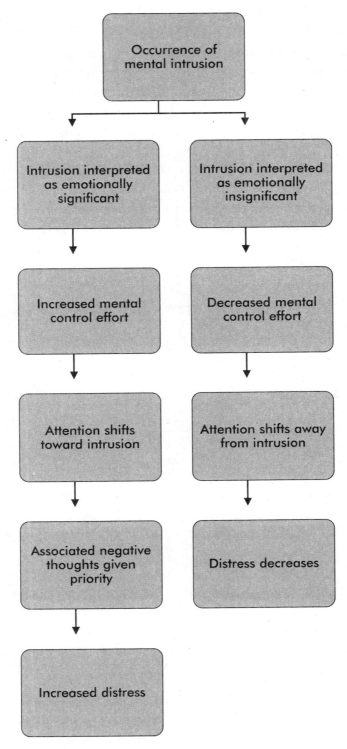

According to this model, you first become mindful of an unwanted intrusive thought, image, or memory. Next you misinterpret the intrusion as a highly significant emotional threat. This leads to excessive efforts to inhibit or suppress the unwanted thought. Paradoxically, your attempts at control actually draw greater attention to the mental intrusion. This sets in motion other negative thought processes like rumination, worry, and obsessive thinking. The result, then, is an increase in personal distress. Of course, there is another possibility, as you can see in figure 3.1: if you had considered the spontaneous intrusion a more neutral or emotionally insignificant mental occurrence, then you'd be less inclined to try and control the thought. As a result, your attention would be drawn away from the intrusion, so your distress would actually decrease.

The next exercise will help you begin to consider how the various mental processes described in the mental-control model might contribute to emotional distress. If you're not yet sure of the personal relevance of this model, you can skip ahead and return to this exercise when you reach the end of the chapter. By then, you'll have a better understanding of your mental responses to intrusive thoughts.

EXERCISE: Start Applying the Mental-Control Model

To help you begin to apply the mental-control model to understand your own distress, answer the questions in the space provided.

1. What intrusive thoughts, images, or memories make you feel distressed?

    _____

    _____

2. What is so emotionally significant or important about the intrusion?

    _____

    _____

3. How are you trying to suppress—that is, not think about—the intrusion?

    _____

    _____

4. What other negative thought processes are involved, such as rumination, worry, and so on?

_____

_____

This exercise represents your first attempt to understand your emotional distress from the mental-control perspective. You may want to return to this exercise to revise your answers after you've completed the remaining exercises in this chapter and have learned more about the components of the mental-control model.

The Mental-Control Perspective

You can gain a deeper understanding of your mental processes by looking at them in terms of each component of the mental-control model. The first element in the model is the occurrence of an unwanted intrusive thought, image, or memory. Learning to detect your unwanted intrusions is the first step in applying the mental-control model to your anxiety, depression or obsessions.

Detecting the Intrusion

The intervention strategies in this workbook require a heightened awareness of problematic intrusive thoughts, images, or memories. While you're probably aware of other negative thinking, such as rumination, worry and self-critical thoughts, these initial intrusive thoughts can be difficult to detect because of their speed and spontaneity. Looking back on the thought-feeling record you completed in chapter 1, were you able to pick out the mental intrusion from the flow of negative thinking? If this proved too difficult, don't be too concerned. The next exercise of keeping a mental-intrusion diary will help improve your awareness.

Cognitive behavioral therapists have long known that keeping a thought diary is important for successful treatment of anxiety and depression (A.T. Beck et al. 1979; J. S. Beck 2011). Using this same approach, the process of breaking down your negative emotional experience into its component parts can help you detect your spontaneous distressing thought, or mental intrusion. Keeping a diary gives you practice in writing about your distress (your negative feelings), the associated circumstance, other negative thinking, and your response or efforts to cope with the distress. By doing this type of structured journaling, the initial mental intrusion becomes clearer. As an example, here's what Samantha's mental-intrusion diary looked like.

Samantha's Mental-Intrusion Diary

Distress Rating: 1 (mild) to 3 (severe)	Circumstance	Awareness of Negative Thinking	Response	Intrusion
anxious (2), guilty, frustrated	Thinking about having to go to a family gathering on the weekend	• Several of my cousins will be there. • I don't know them very well. • My parents will expect me to socialize with the cousins. • The last family gathering was so stressful. • I remember getting really flushed in the face and clamming up.	• I ended up leaving the conversation with my cousins and sitting with my parents and older relatives. • I pretended to feel sick and left early.	1. I'm going to feel intensely anxious and uncomfortable.
anxious (3), stressed, depressed	Thinking about a group project meeting I must attend	• I don't really know these people. • I'll be expected to contribute to the conversation about the project. • I'll probably get flushed in the face and start to tremble. • Everyone will notice I'm anxious and wonder what's wrong with me. • I just hate these group projects.	• I'll have to go and endure the pain.	2. I'm about to face one of the worst days in my life.

Samantha recorded two distressing experiences that involved a surge of anxiety. Both times, the anxiety was associated with anticipating a future social interaction. Samantha's first anxious experience involved thinking about going to a family gathering. Notice that she rated her main emotion, anxiety, as moderate. She was aware of a stream of negative thinking that involved how she might feel while interacting with her cousins, who were all within her age range. From this, Samantha was able to identify the initial unwanted intrusive thought that ignited this fresh round of anticipatory anxiety: the expectation of experiencing an intolerable state of anxiety. When she followed the same self-monitoring process on the second occasion, she discovered a similar mental intrusion. It was clear that Samantha's distress was often triggered by sudden anticipatory thoughts that she would have another bout of awful anxiety. No wonder her automatic response was to try to minimize the influence of anxiety on her life.

Now it's your turn. Recall a recent upsetting experience and use the next exercise to detect your mental intrusion.

EXERCISE: Your Mental-Intrusion Diary

Starting in the column on the left, record the type of distress and intensity of negative emotion you experienced (such as feeling sad, anxious, angry, guilty, and so on), and rate it as 1 for mild, 2 for moderate, or 3 for severe. Next, briefly describe the circumstance that led to the distress, any negative thinking you were immediately aware of, and your response, or how you dealt with the distress. From this information, deduce the initial intrusive thought, and record it in the space to the right of the table. If you need additional space, you can visit http://www.newharbinger.com/38426 to download copies of this mental-intrusion diary.

Mental-Intrusion Diary

Distress Rating: 1 (mild) to 3 (severe)	Circumstance	Awareness of Negative Thinking	Response	Intrusion
				1. _____
				_____
				_____
				1. _____
				_____
				_____
				1. _____
				_____
				_____

Intrusion

1. _____
_____
_____

2. _____
_____
_____

1. _____
_____
_____

Distress Rating: 1 (mild) to 3 (severe)	Circumstance	Awareness of Negative Thinking	Response

You'll want to make or download several copies of the mental-intrusion diary so you can continue to monitor your distressing thoughts and feelings. The more distressing experiences you record in the diary, the more skilled you'll get at detecting the initial unwanted mental intrusion responsible for your distress. Look for patterns in your intrusive thinking. Is the same intrusive thought happening repeatedly? Are you experiencing any particular intrusive images or memories when feeling anxious or depressed? When getting started, don't worry about the accuracy of your recordings. You'll get better at identifying these initial negative thoughts with practice.

If you are still having difficulty monitoring your negative thoughts and feelings, you can use the following probes to help discover the critical intrusive thoughts associated with your distress.

DISTRESS

We are usually more aware of our feelings than our thoughts, so it's helpful to begin by asking, *What am I feeling at this moment?* If the emotion is sadness, the intrusive thought will likely deal with personal loss or failure; if it is anxiety, the intrusion will likely focus on threat or danger; if it is guilt, the intrusion will likely center on personal wrongdoing; and if you're feeling angry, the unwanted mental intrusion will likely represent perceived injustice or unfairness.

CIRCUMSTANCE

Next ask yourself, *What is happening around me that's so upsetting?* Often our intrusive thoughts are triggered by the events, people, and situations we encounter. Whatever you are doing at any moment will influence what you think.

OTHER NEGATIVE THOUGHTS

Often we are aware of negative thinking when anxious or depressed, but these thoughts occur in response to the initial intrusion. Ask yourself, *What have I been thinking over the last few minutes?* By writing down these known negative thoughts, you can trace your pattern of thinking back to the most likely theme of the intrusion.

RESPONSE

How did I react or try to deal with the distress? is the final self-reflective question. How you attempted to deal with the distress can indicate the type of intrusive thought that initiated the anxious or depressive experience.

The mental-intrusion diary is one of the main assessment tools in the mental-control approach to negative emotion. You'll be using this diary as a clinical tool for tracking the frequency of mental intrusions and distress. Your skill at intrusion detection will improve the more you use the mental-intrusion diary. If you're continuing to have difficulty self-monitoring your unwanted thoughts and feelings, it might be helpful to review chapter 1 to refresh your understanding of intrusive thinking. If you've succeeded in identifying at least one or two problematic intrusions, you're ready to tackle the second step in the mental-control approach: to discover how the importance placed on the intrusion affects your level of anxiety, depression, or other negative emotion.

A Matter of Importance

One of the main tasks of our brain is to sort through a bombardment of intended and unintended thought to determine which are most important to our well-being and survival. We are doing this sorting and classifying continuously with both automatic (unconscious) and more effortful (conscious) mental processes, which leads to the assignment of attentional priority to our thoughts. One of the most useful rules of information processing is that we pay attention to the thoughts we consider most important to our physical and emotional well-being.

For example, let's say you're doing something useful, and suddenly the thought pops into your mind: *Don't forget tomorrow's early morning meeting with the manager*. Instantly, you stop what you're doing and enter the appointment in your calendar, possibly programming an alert, so you won't forget it. Then you go back to the task at hand. What just happened in this example? Suddenly you had an intrusive thought about the early morning meeting. You immediately paid attention to this intrusion because you evaluated the thought as highly significant. You don't usually have early morning meetings with your manager, and so there was a high probability you'd forget it if you didn't write it down. Given that the company was in the process of downsizing, you knew it was in your best interest not to miss the appointment.

So how do we decide when an intrusive thought is so significant that we should pay close attention to it? There are actually five criteria that determine the personal significance of a thought: personal threat, responsibility, negative effects, unexpectedness, and need to control. The best way to understand how these criteria determine thought significance is to work on one of the intrusive thoughts associated with your distress.

EXERCISE: Interpretation-of-Significance Worksheet

Go back to your mental-intrusion diary and select an unwanted mental intrusion you identified with your distress. Write the intrusion in the space below:

_____

_____

Next, respond to these questions about the intrusion.

1. Do you associate a personal threat or a bad outcome with the intrusion? Describe the threat or negative consequence here:

   _____

   _____

2. Do you feel responsible for preventing this negative consequence? If so, explain how you are responsible:

   _____

   _____

3. Do you believe having the intrusive thought could have a negative effect on you or others? If so, explain how this would happen:

   _____

   _____

4. Does the intrusion seem more significant because it happens frequently and is distressing? Answer yes or no:

   _____

5. Is it important that you suppress, or not think about, the intrusive thought? If yes, explain what might happen if you lost control of the thought:

   _____

   _____

Your answers to these five questions explain why the intrusive thought has gained such personal significance. Given its importance, can you now understand why it grabs your attention when it pops into your mind? This interpretation of significance plays a key role in causing an escalation in your distressing thoughts and feelings. We all automatically pay more attention and respond more vigorously to thoughts, images, memories, or other ideas that we consider important in our lives.

You can visit http://www.newharbinger.com/38426 to download other copies of this interpretation-of-significance worksheet, so you can use it as a checklist with other distressing thoughts. The mental-control perspective on anxiety and depression teaches you how to reduce the significance attributed to these disturbing intrusive thoughts. And you'll soon be doing a lot of work on how to change your interpretation of them. In the meantime, consider how Samantha misinterpreted the significance of her intrusive thought *I'm going to feel intensely anxious and uncomfortable.*

Samantha considered the intrusive thought personally threatening because feeling anxious in social situations was just about the worst thing she could imagine. She held herself responsible for concealing the anxiety from others. She also believed that having the intrusive thought before a social event actually increased the likelihood that she'd feel anxious at the event. She viewed her anticipatory intrusive thoughts as a way of *priming the anxiety pump.* Although most people wonder if they'll feel anxious at an unfamiliar social event, Samantha believed that the sheer frequency of her anxious intrusions reflected their unusual importance in her life. In fact, Samantha became convinced that eliminating the anticipatory intrusive thoughts was a key to reducing her anxiety in social situations. As a result, intrusive thoughts of *being anxious* became one of the most significant threats in Samantha's life.

So far, this chapter has focused on two key components in the vicious cycle of emotional distress: the occurrence of unwanted mental intrusions and the misinterpretation of their significance. The final component from the mental-control perspective is a heightened effort to directly suppress unwanted distressing thoughts.

Intentional Mental Control

Once an unwanted intrusive thought is considered a highly significant threat, it's natural to try hard not to think about it (see figure 3.1). If you think back to the white-bear experiment in chapter 2, remember that efforts to actively inhibit an unwanted thought make you more susceptible to the mental-control paradox. Increased efforts at avoidance draw even more attention to the unwanted thought. Once your attention is focused on a particular negative intrusive thought, other types of thinking, like worry and rumination, that are consistent with the intrusive thought content, will also gain importance and flood your mind. You become trapped in an ever more complex web of unhealthy thinking. The end result is an increase in distress, which then primes more negative intrusive thoughts, setting in motion a vicious cycle of emotional disturbance. No wonder anxiety, depression, guilt, and other negative emotions can seem like a speeding runaway train, impossible to control.

When looking at your own efforts at intentional mental control, there are two characteristics that must be considered. First, how hard are you trying to inhibit the unwanted thinking? And second, what actual strategies do you use to gain control over unwanted thoughts and feelings? To understand why mental control seems to be failing, it's important to understand how each of these characteristics plays out when you have a distressing intrusive thought.

HEIGHTENED MENTAL-CONTROL EFFORT

Effort is a critical feature of self-control. You can put a lot of effort or none at all into controlling your intrusive thoughts. The next exercise will help you evaluate what you are doing now.

EXERCISE: How Hard Do You Try to Inhibit Intrusions?

To determine your mental-control effort, review the intrusive thoughts recorded in your mental-intrusion diary. Then respond to these questions in terms of your experience with unwanted intrusions.

1. In comparison to other thoughts that pop into your mind, how much effort do you put into actively inhibiting distressing intrusive thoughts? How hard do you try not to think about the mental intrusion? Place a checkmark (√) next to one of these responses:

    _____ Try really hard

    _____ Try moderately hard

    _____ Put slight effort into thought inhibition

    _____ Do not try to inhibit the intrusion

2. How often do you engage in active mental control of intrusive thoughts? Place a checkmark (√) next to one of these responses:

    _____ Every time I have the intrusion

    _____ Only when I'm feeling distressed or upset

_____ *Usually I don't try to control the intrusion*

_____ *I never try to control the intrusion*

3. How difficult would it be to completely stop efforts to inhibit, dismiss, or not think about your distressing intrusive thoughts? Place a checkmark (√) next to one of these responses:

_____ *Almost impossible*

_____ *Very difficult*

_____ *Somewhat difficult*

_____ *Not at all difficult*

If you were inclined to check one of the first two options in this set of questions, it's likely you are putting considerable effort into mental control.

The more invested you are in mental controllability, the greater the risk of falling victim to the paradox of mental control. To help you overcome this problem, this workbook places a great deal of emphasis on learning to let go of intentional control efforts. Chapter 5 offers exercises that will help you learn to be more accepting and less invested in suppressing unwanted mental intrusions. In the meantime, being aware that you may be overextending yourself in the pursuit of mental control is another important step in transforming your approach to unwanted thoughts and feelings.

MENTAL-CONTROL STRATEGIES

It's also important to consider the strategies that you use to inhibit unwanted intrusive thoughts. Research shows that once a mental intrusion is deemed highly significant, it's only natural to use some strategy to divert attention away from the thought (Clark, Purdon, and Byers 2000; Wegner and Pennebaker 1993). So what mental-control strategies do you use to shut down thinking that's making you feel anxious, depressed, guilty, or frustrated? The next exercise will help you figure this out.

First you'll need to review your entries in your mental-intrusion diary as well as the thought-feeling record in chapter 1. As you consider your experiences with unwanted thoughts and feelings, can you remember your response to those episodes and what you did to help yourself feel better?

EXERCISE: The Mental-Control Strategies Questionnaire

Consider your experiences with distressing intrusive thoughts and feelings. Then, on a scale of 0 to 2, where 0 is never, 1 is occasionally, and 2 is frequently, rate how often you used each strategy listed here. Also rate how you perceived the effectiveness of each strategy, where 0 is not effective, 1 is somewhat effective, and 2 is very effective.

Control Strategy	Estimated Frequency			Estimated Effectiveness		
1. Replace with another thought.	0	1	2	0	1	2
2. Try to reason with yourself.	0	1	2	0	1	2
3. Criticize yourself for thinking this way.	0	1	2	0	1	2
4. Seek reassurance from others.	0	1	2	0	1	2
5. Tell yourself to stop thinking this way.	0	1	2	0	1	2
6. Engage in an activity to distract yourself.	0	1	2	0	1	2
7. Analyze the meaning, why you are thinking like this.	0	1	2	0	1	2
8. Look for evidence that refutes the intrusive thought.	0	1	2	0	1	2
9. Repeat a phrase or action (for example, checking something) that counters (neutralizes) the thought or reduces distress.	0	1	2	0	1	2
10. Actively suppress thinking about the intrusion.	0	1	2	0	1	2
11. Just accept the thought, let it float through your mind without engaging the intrusion.	0	1	2	0	1	2
12. Try to reinterpret the intrusion as a more positive, helpful thought.	0	1	2	0	1	2
13. Try to relax, meditate, or breathe slowly.	0	1	2	0	1	2

14. Find humor in the situation.	0	1	2	0	1	2
15. Pray or focus on a comforting phrase or idea.	0	1	2	0	1	2
16. Try to reassure yourself that everything will be fine.	0	1	2	0	1	2
17. Perform a compulsive ritual (repeatedly wash hands, check, redo, or repeat actions).	0	1	2	0	1	2
18. Avoid things that might trigger the unwanted intrusion.	0	1	2	0	1	2

Based on your questionnaire responses, which mental-control strategies are you using most to deal with unwanted thoughts and feelings? Are you relying on effective or ineffective strategies? Are you surprised at the limited extent of your mental-control skills? If you previously concluded that you tend to put a lot of effort into mental control and now you realize your actual control strategies are not very effective, do you now understand why the paradox of mental control is working against you?

Your assessment of your current state of mental self-control will be valuable in determining how to apply the new self-control skills that this workbook will introduce later. It is entirely possible that your anxiety, depression, or obsessions have persisted because you are exerting too much effort with relatively ineffective self-control strategies. But there is hope if you read on! This workbook was designed to help people reverse their sense of helplessness when facing distressing thoughts and feelings.

Before you begin to work on improving your self-control, however, it's important to integrate all the assessment work you've done in this chapter into a mental-control profile that will guide your work in subsequent chapters.

Your Mental-Control Profile

This chapter started with a story about how easy it is to get lost in unfamiliar places without a map or some kind of guidance system. Now it's time to construct a mental-control road map that will guide you through the remaining exercises in this workbook. To help you stay on course, the mental-control profile in the next exercise will help you integrate all the assessment information you've collected in this chapter. It's based on the mental-control model in figure 3.1.

EXERCISE: Your Mental-Control Profile

Use the four text boxes to describe the various mental processes involved in your emotional distress. Begin by writing down the most important unwanted mental intrusions from the mental-intrusions diary. In the next box, write a brief narrative on what makes these intrusions personally significant. You can base this description on the answers you provided in the interpretation-of-significance exercise. Then list the mental-control strategies you use with the intrusions by selecting the strategies you circled the most in the mental-control strategies questionnaire. Finally, consider other negative thinking that characterizes your experiences of distress. For example, are there particular concerns that you worry or ruminate on, or do you experience other thoughts of self-criticalness, threat, vulnerability, or blame? Note these in the final text box.

Your Mental-Control Profile

Unwanted Intrusive Thoughts, Images, or Memories

1. _____

2. _____

3. _____

4. _____

Interpretation of Emotional Significance

_____

_____

_____

Mental-Control Strategies

1. _____   2. _____

3. _____   4. _____

5. _____   6. _____

Other Negative Thought Processes

1. _____

2. _____

3. _____

The work you've done on creating a mental-control profile helps you better understand which mental processes are contributing to your emotional distress. Using your mental-control profile as a guide, you will be able to use more effectively the new intervention strategies presented in subsequent chapters to reverse the adverse effects of failed mental control.

Wrap-Up

You can think of this chapter as a guided tour of your mind. If you have rushed through it because you are eager to jump into the intervention strategies in upcoming chapters, I encourage you to take a little extra time with this chapter before moving on. You'll find the upcoming intervention strategies more helpful if you have taken time with the mental-control profile to assess your intrusions and their control. In fact, this is so important that you may want to go back and do any exercises that you skipped or redo any to which you gave little attention. It will unlock a self-discovery process that will make subsequent chapters much more meaningful.

To review, here are some of the key points outlined in this chapter:

- Unwanted intrusive thoughts, their interpretation, and heightened efforts to inhibit distressing thoughts and feelings are critical mental processes in the persistence of emotional distress.

- Learning to be more aware of unwanted mental intrusions associated with experiences of anxiety, depression, or other negative emotion is the first step in developing a mental-control perspective on distress.

- When you evaluate unwanted intrusive thinking as a highly significant mental incursion, you will focus greater attention on these thoughts, images, and memories.

- Your self-assessment of the importance of mental control and its strategies highlights how the paradox of mental control contributes to emotional distress.

- Constructing a personal mental-control profile will increase your success with the workbook by focusing the intervention strategies on the most important features of your negative thoughts and feelings.

With your completed assessment tools and your mental-control profile in hand, it's time to start dealing more effectively with your distressing intrusive thoughts and feelings. Chapter 4 explains how you can minimize the personal significance of distressing mental intrusions, so you begin to treat them like common spontaneous thought. We can call this *mental detoxification*, a process that strips the distressing intrusion of the heightened meaning and significance noted in your mental-control profile. When great personal significance is attached to an unwanted thought, your attention will be drawn to it, so it becomes a more powerful and disturbing idea. Detoxification is a critical intervention in reforming your mental-control approach to the distressing intrusions you discovered in this chapter.

CHAPTER 4

Control Skills: Mental Detoxification

Can a thought be toxic? In brief, yes. Certain maladaptive ways of coping can turn negative intrusive thoughts, images, or memories into frequent, highly distressing cognitions that are toxic for your well-being. This is what happens when we misinterpret the significance of our unwanted mental intrusions. When we overestimate their emotional significance, we are more likely to lose control of them. We turn some types of common spontaneous thought into toxic mental flotsam that can wreak emotional havoc on our daily lives.

This chapter focuses on the misinterpretation of significance that characterizes anxious and depressive intrusions. You'll learn how to reevaluate their significance, so you can take a more effective approach to unwanted distressing thoughts and feelings. This process is called *detoxification* because you eliminate the toxic nature of your negative thinking as you realign its perceived significance. More specifically, mental detoxification is the process of learning to accept the intrusion for what it really is: a spontaneous, unintended thought, image, or memory that has less personal significance because it can be considered the product of a highly imaginative brain. But before you learn how to detoxify your distressing thoughts, meet Claire, a woman in her mid-fifties, who was struggling with intense anxiety and worry over an impending surgery to repair an abdominal aortic aneurysm. You'll see how Claire's anxiety was fueled by the emotional significance of her intrusive thoughts about the surgery.

Claire's Story: Facing Her Greatest Fear

Claire was worried about dying. She had never before faced major surgery, and just thinking about it terrified her. The surgery was constantly on her mind. Everything reminded her of the surgery, and the thoughts always focused on some catastrophic outcome. She'd have an image of herself lying on the operating table with doctors and nurses frantically working to save her life. She had thoughts of the surgeon telling her the operation was unsuccessful, or she'd suddenly think about the postoperative pain. She could imagine her husband and adult children being shaken as they're told she hadn't survived the operation. These unwanted mental intrusions set off a firestorm of worry in Claire's mind. The anxiety would build to the point where she couldn't sleep, eat, or socialize. The surgery-related intrusions became so toxic that Claire felt like she was losing control over her own mind and emotions. Her doctor had warned her that high preoperative anxiety would slow down her postoperative recovery, so Claire knew she had to get a grip over her thinking, but how?

Toxic and Nontoxic Mental Intrusions

The first step in mental detoxification is to be clear on the unwanted thought, image, or memory that is most responsible for your anxiety, depression, or other negative emotion. This is your *toxic intrusion*. For Claire, any sudden, unwanted thought of the surgery was toxic, so she realized that her toxic intrusion could be summed up like this: *This surgery will be the worst day of my life.*

EXERCISE: Name a Toxic Negative Intrusion

You've been tracking your unwanted thoughts and feelings with the mental-intrusion diary in chapter 3, so consult what you recorded in the intrusion column to select a thought you consider especially emotionally upsetting. Choose one that does the following:

1. Repeatedly triggers feelings of anxiety, depression, or other distress

2. Is highly distressing

3. Elicits strong efforts of mental inhibition or suppression

4. Activates a stream of other negative thinking like worry or rumination

Write your toxic intrusion here:

_____

_____

The next step in the detoxification process is to identify a negative intrusive thought, image, or memory that you don't find particularly distressing: a *nontoxic intrusion*. At first, you might think that you don't have any nondistressing negative thoughts; that all your negative thoughts are upsetting. But, in reality, all of us experience negative intrusions that we don't find distressing. For example, Claire had a daughter, Mary, who was unhappy about her employment situation. Claire would often have an intrusive thought about Mary's unhappiness with her job, but this thought didn't upset her. Instead, she would remind herself that Mary is young and will eventually find a better job.

EXERCISE: Name a Nontoxic Negative Intrusion

Choose a negative nondistressing intrusive thought that you've had recently. Maybe you've had an argument with a coworker and then have intrusive thoughts about the argument several hours later. The argument was definitely unpleasant and your intrusive thoughts about it are negative, but you're not feeling unduly distressed by the situation. In this case, you're treating your intrusive reminders of the argument as normal unpleasant thoughts, that is, nontoxic intrusive thinking.

If you find it challenging to discover a negative but nondistressing intrusive thought, here are some questions that may help:

1. Are there any specific problems, situations, or concerns in your life that are unpleasant but not personally distressing? Think about something unpleasant but fairly common, like a minor stressor or daily hassle, such as a disagreement with someone, being late for a meeting or appointment, paying bills, feeling slightly unwell or tired, or some annoyance at your spouse or children.

2. What do you think about when spontaneously reminded of the unpleasant situation? What thoughts pop into your mind about the minor problem or negative situation?

3. When your mind wanders or you're daydreaming about this problem or unpleasant situation, what are you thinking?

Write the nontoxic negative intrusion here:

_____

_____

If you still have difficulty coming up with a nondistressing negative intrusion, you can use the mental-intrusion diary introduced in chapter 3 to monitor negative intrusions associated with minor daily annoyances or hassles. If you use the diary over several days, you'll probably catch a number of common stressful experiences that trigger some negative thinking. These negative thoughts would be examples of nontoxic negative intrusions as long as you don't find them particularly distressing.

It's important to complete these two exercises before proceeding to the next step in the mental detoxification process. For the other exercises in this chapter, you'll need to have both a toxic and a nontoxic negative intrusion to work on. If you're still struggling with this discovery task, you could ask your spouse or close friend for some advice. Or if you're seeing a mental health therapist or a counselor, your therapist could use a therapeutic strategy called *guided discovery* to help you identify these two types of thinking in your daily life.

Toxic Intrusion: Interpretations of Significance

The next step in the detoxification process is to look back at your toxic intrusion and write a short narrative on what's so personally significant or important about this unwanted thought, image, or memory. This is a called a *toxic significance narrative*. Here is the toxic significance narrative that Claire wrote while doing this exercise:

> *I know I'm responsible for these fearful intrusive thoughts about the surgery. But the more I keep having the intrusions, the more convinced I am that something terrible is going to happen, such as dying on the operating table. Nothing is more important in my life right now than this surgery, but the more I keep having these terrible intrusive thoughts, the more convinced I am they could be a bad omen, a sign of terrible times ahead. I know I've got to stop thinking this way, because it's making me more anxious, which can't be a good emotional state when you're facing surgery. The intrusions remind me that the future is so uncertain, but it's this feeling of uncertainty that bothers me most. All of this makes the spontaneous thoughts about surgery the most important and personally upsetting thing that I can think about right now. I've tried everything to calm my mind, but nothing works. Nothing could be more important than to get a better grip on my mental health.*

As you begin to work on your toxic-significance narrative, don't worry if you can't be as detailed in your narrative as Claire was. It can be challenging to find the right words to describe what is so emotionally significant about a toxic intrusive thought. Ask yourself, *What's so significant about this intrusive thought that I pay so much attention to it and try so hard not to think about it?* You may also want to return to chapter 3 to review what you wrote about toxic intrusions in the interpretation-of-significance exercise and in your mental-control profile.

EXERCISE: Your Toxic-Significance Narrative

Think about why your negative thought, image, or memory is so important. As you look back to your last experience with the unwanted distressing intrusion, answer the following questions:

1. Does the intrusive thought cause you to question something about yourself, that is, the type of person you are?

2. Do you think that having the thought increases the likelihood of some negative future outcome for you or your loved ones?

3. Does the intrusion remind you of some horrible or regretful event in the past?

4. How does the intrusive thought affect real-life circumstances and experiences?

5. Why is it so important to inhibit or suppress the intrusive thought?

Write your toxic significance narrative in the space provided.

_____

_____

_____

_____

_____

Were you able to describe what makes the unwanted intrusion so significant or meaningful? If you were able to give a detailed account, that's great. But if the only thing you could come up with for your narrative is that the intrusion makes you feel upset, that's also fine for now.

Often what makes a thought important to us is its perceived negative effect. You're acknowledging that the intrusion is a significant threat because of how it makes you feel. Because you feel this way, you're compelled to pay attention to it and try to control it, but then you fail and so the thought grows in significance and distress. Later in the chapter, you'll start learning how to detoxify your distressing thoughts, but first it will help to examine how you tend to interpret negative thoughts that do not distress you.

Nontoxic Intrusion: Interpretations of Insignificance

The next step is to examine the nondistressing negative intrusion that you named earlier in the chapter and focus on why you've concluded that this intrusion is personally insignificant. In this case, you're making an interpretation of insignificance. You're telling yourself, *Look, it's okay to think this way. It's perfectly normal to have thoughts like this. Nothing bad will happen to me; these thoughts will eventually stop.* When you generate this neutral interpretation of a negative intrusion, you are essentially normalizing the thought. You conclude that the negative intrusion is nontoxic. You might treat it as trivial or even meaningless.

As an example of neutral interpretation, here is what Claire wrote when she examined her thoughts about her daughter's dissatisfaction at work:

> *I feel bad that Mary is unhappy with her job, but I know there is nothing I can do about it. I remind myself she is a young, well-educated woman and that it is not uncommon for even the most talented people to start out in a job they don't like. She'll probably find a better job eventually. Lots of people live well even when they are unhappy with their current work. Me thinking about Mary's employment unhappiness will not help her with this problem. We can never be certain about the direction our life will take. In fact, this is one of the great advantages of being young; there are still many years ahead to try new ventures. In the end, controlling the intrusive thought is immaterial, because whether I think about Mary's employment or not, it changes nothing.*

The example of Claire's nondistressing interpretation may help you generate an interpretation of insignificance for your own negative intrusive thought. Note that Claire's thoughts about her daughter's dissatisfaction with her current employment are definitely unintended intrusive thoughts, and they focus on a negative issue; however, Claire didn't feel upset when she was reminded of her daughter's employment dissatisfaction. This was because she didn't consider the thought to be a significant emotional threat. She was able to normalize the negative intrusion.

The next exercise will help you discover how you've arrived at a neutral, or insignificant, interpretation of a nontoxic mental intrusion.

EXERCISE: Your Nontoxic Insignificance Narrative

Review your nontoxic negative intrusion from the earlier exercise in this chapter. Then use the following questions as a guide to discover why you've concluded this negative intrusion is not personally significant.

1. Did you perceive that the intrusive thought had no implication for the future, whether positive or negative?

2. Did you conclude there was no connection between the imagined intrusive thought and real-life experience, that is, that the thought did not determine your experience?

3. Did you realize that there was little you could do about the thought or that you had little or no responsibility for what thoughts popped into your mind?

4. Did you decide there was no sense in trying to suppress or inhibit the intrusive thought, since it had no influence on real life?

5. Did you conclude the intrusive thought had no personal relevance to you, or that it meant nothing about the type of person you are?

Write your nontoxic insignificance narrative in the space provided:

_____

_____

_____

_____

_____

Were you able to produce a clear narrative of why your nontoxic mental intrusion was insignificant?

You may be wondering why I've been emphasizing how nondistressing mental intrusions are interpreted. After all, it's the distressing, toxic intrusions that are responsible for your anxiety and depression. But there are a couple of reasons why discovering nontoxic interpretations is important to the mental detoxification intervention. First, it serves as a good reminder that you don't overreact to every negative thought that pops into your mind. Rather there are many occasions when you have an unpleasant thought or memory and you evaluate the thought in a perfectly rational, healthy manner. If you can do that with your nontoxic intrusions, you'll be able to use the same approach when the distressing thought pops into your mind. And second, you can use your work in this exercise as the standard for determining whether you're making adaptive or maladaptive interpretations. It can be your prototype, a type of mental yardstick, to determine how far you've strayed from treating a distressing intrusive thought as a normal, nonthreatening way of thinking.

Now that you've identified the problematic interpretation of the toxic intrusion and the more normalized, benign interpretation associated with a nondistressing negative thought, you can begin to use these insights to detoxify your troubling thoughts.

The Toxification Process

By now you realize that when a negative thought pops into your mind, its fate depends on whether you consider it a significant emotional threat or a normal, benign random thought. This means that any thought can become distressing if interpreted in a threatening way. In fact, there is probably someone who is very distressed by the same negative thought that is not distressing to you. So you could ask the question, how might someone troubled by your non-toxic negative intrusion interpret it in a meaningful and threatening manner?

The next exercise requires some imagination. It asks you to turn your nontoxic intrusive thought into a distressing mental experience. As an example of how to do this, here is how Claire reinterpreted the significance of her earlier negative thought about her daughter's unemployment:

> When I have the intrusive thought about Mary's employment, I feel upset if I think to myself, "What if Mary never finds a fulfilling job and has to spend the rest of her life working for this miserable company? Her unhappiness and discouragement about work could ruin her life, possibly even drive her into a clinical depression." The fact that I keep having these intrusive thoughts must mean something. Maybe it's a premonition that things are not going to work out for Mary. Maybe I should be doing more to comfort her, maybe give her advice on how to handle an unhappy job situation. After all, I am her mother. It's hard not knowing what will happen with Mary; I have this queasy feeling it's not going to turn out well for her. I need to do something to address these intrusive thoughts. If I don't do something to stop thinking like this, I won't be able to have peace of mind; besides Mary could really use my help now.

It is easy to see from Claire's hypothetical interpretation how she was able to turn a benign intrusive thought into something very distressing. All she did was reinterpret the intrusion as a threat, as a sign that Mary wouldn't succeed. Notice she appraised the thought as a sign that she needed to do something to help Mary. The intrusion also reminded her of feeling anxious about the uncertainty of life and that the thought itself was a premonition of future unhappiness for Mary. She concluded that she needed to pay attention to this intrusive thought: she needed to exercise some control over it. In the end, it is easy to see how this interpretation would turn the unhappy thought about her daughter's unemployment into a toxic mental intrusion.

You might be hesitant to do this exercise because the last thing you want is to intentionally create another distressing thought. However, this probably won't happen, since what you are generating is only a hypothetical scenario. I encourage you to spend some time on this. It will be well worth your time and effort.

EXERCISE: How to Create Distress

Look back at your nontoxic negative intrusion and imagine how a different interpretation of the same thought could create distress. Generate a hypothetical interpretation of significance for your nontoxic negative mental intrusion. Here are some ways to think about the intrusion that could make it more upsetting:

1. Exaggerate the negative, threatening, or upsetting possibilities associated with the intrusive thought.

2. Focus on how you could be personally responsible for everything associated with the intrusion.

3. Convince yourself that the repeated occurrence of the thought means that it's important and deserves your utmost attention.

4. Imagine that having this intrusive thought increases the likelihood of a negative outcome for you or your loved ones.

5. Be convinced that you need to suppress or inhibit the intrusive thought, or that if you fail in your mental-control efforts, your anxiety or other negative emotions will worsen.

Write down your hypothetical distressing interpretation of the nontoxic intrusion:

_____

_____

_____

_____

_____

Were you able to come up with a hypothetical distressing interpretation of your negative thought? This exercise is useful because it provides further insight into the importance of the interpretation process.

One of the main ways to turn a negative thought into a distressing one is to imagine terrible consequences for yourself or others if you continue to dwell on the unwanted thought. This is a form of *catastrophizing*. It could go something like this: *I've got to stop thinking like this, or I'll drive myself crazy*; or *If I don't stop thinking like this, I'll get more depressed*; or *My life will be ruined*. Reacting to a thought as if it were a catastrophe is a sure way to create a highly significant emotional threat.

Detoxifying Your Distressing Thoughts

You've now arrived at the heart of the mental detoxification intervention. From the previous exercises, you've seen that interpreting a negative thought as an emotionally significant threat increases its distressing quality. You've also seen that reacting to a negative intrusion as an insignificant, benign, normal mental occurrence reduces its associated distress. The challenge, then, is to change how you understand or interpret the unwanted thoughts, images, or memories that characterize your anxiety, depression, or obsessionality. The therapeutic intervention of mental detoxification is a self-control skill that transforms a significant negative intrusion into an insignificant mental occurrence.

The detoxification process consists of three steps that will help you develop a new understanding of your distressing intrusive thought, image, or memory:

1. Decatastrophize the consequence.

2. Reality-test the connection you're making between your intrusion and daily life.

3. Write a detoxification narrative.

You'll want to use all three steps to detoxify distressing mental intrusions that are associated with your anxiety or depression. You'll learn how to take these steps in the next three exercises. It's time to begin the process of stripping these distressing intrusions of their significance and meaning.

Decatastrophizing

A series of questions in this first exercise will help you discover a different perspective on the consequences of a distressing intrusive thought:

1. What's the real probability that the catastrophe, the worst-case outcome, will happen?

2. Are there any positive aspects to the intrusive thought that you're overlooking?

3. Is there evidence that the intrusive thought is only mildly distressing and quite tolerable?

The goal is to redefine the implications of the unwanted thought in a more realistic, normal fashion.

When Claire considered the first of these questions, the probability that she would die from her surgery, she immediately realized that she was catastrophizing. She was treating the intrusive thought as if she had a fifty-fifty chance of survival when the actual survival and recovery rates were much higher. So Claire readjusted her estimate of a catastrophic outcome to match with the known medical facts. Next she asked the second question: had she been overlooking any positive aspects to her intrusive thought? The answer was yes: she could use intrusive thoughts about her surgery as a reminder of some practical steps she needed to take to prepare for the surgery. For example, she could expect a ten-to-fourteen-day stay in the hospital and would need help with household chores for several weeks afterward. So instead of trying to push the surgery intrusions from her mind, she focused her attention on what she needed to do to get ready for her hospitalization. Finally, she worked on reinterpreting the intrusion as only mildly distressing. For example, she wrote that it's completely normal to dread surgery; that no one likes the pain and limitation in functioning that goes with weeks of recovery. She also reminded herself that the surgery was a solution to a real-life health problem; that is, the abdominal aneurysm. So instead of treating the surgery intrusion as representing the worst day in her life, she realized it represented one of the most hopeful days of her life. It was an answer to a medical problem that could end her life prematurely if not dealt with.

EXERCISE: Decatastrophize the Consequence

Go back to the first exercise in this chapter, where you named a toxic intrusion. Write it down here.

Now read each question to probe your understanding of this intrusion's consequence. Write your answer, giving your decatastrophized, more realistic perspective. Your answers should present a more benign way to think about the unwanted intrusion.

What's the real probability that the catastrophe, the worst-case outcome will happen? Basing your more realistic estimate on hard facts—what you've really experienced and not on what you imagine could happen—write down the actual probability that this catastrophe will occur:

_____

_____

_____

Are there any positive aspects to the intrusive thought that you're overlooking? Could these positive features mean that the thought is more normal and less threatening than you've assumed? Write about any positive elements that you can associate with the intrusive thought:

_____

_____

_____

Is there evidence that the intrusive thought is only mildly distressing and quite tolerable? Write down some of the less distressing possible outcomes:

_____

_____

_____

Were you able to successfully decatastrophize the thought? Maybe you were able to generate a less catastrophic, more realistic outcome, but you are finding it hard to believe. Don't worry about that for now. It's important for you to at least realize that there is a less troubling way to view the intrusions. The next exercise will help strengthen your belief in the decatastrophized narrative.

After completing the decatastrophizing exercise, the next step is to deal directly with the intrusive thought. Even after doing this exercise, it can be hard to reject the view that having the unwanted thought increases the likelihood that something bad will happen in real life. For example, Claire wondered if the intrusive thoughts about her surgery were a type of premonition: because she was thinking about the surgery so much and getting so upset, maybe this meant catastrophe was more likely to happen.

Reality Check

If you believe there's a strong connection between the intrusive thought and what will happen in real life, you'll automatically assume the thought is highly important. However, if you can accept that intrusive thoughts that pop into your head are the product of your imaginative brain, with no direct causal link to negative events in the real world, then you can downgrade the significance of the intrusion.

When Claire examined the connection between her surgery intrusions and her everyday experience, she realized the two were quite separate. She could have an intrusive thought about the surgery almost anywhere and at any time of day. For example, she might be out shopping and start thinking about the surgery, or she could be watching TV or even talking to a friend when the surgery intrusion would pop into her mind. It was as if her mind were on a single track regardless of her everyday experience. The intrusion was also clearly the product of her imagination. Sometimes she'd imagine herself in the operating room or lying in a hospital bed. She could imagine what the aneurysm looked like in her body. Claire took this as evidence that these intrusive thoughts were simply a product of a very active imagination.

EXERCISE: Give the Connection a Reality Test

Correct any faulty connections you've drawn between the intrusive thought and real-life consequences. Read the questions below to probe the intrusion's connection to real life. Write your answers in the space provided to make a realistic thought-event connection.

Is there any past experience that indicates the intrusive thought caused a negative or unwanted experience? Write down the evidence that the intrusive thought was unrelated to your everyday experience:

_____

_____

_____

Is there any evidence that the intrusive thought is a product of your imagination? Write down evidence that your intrusive thoughts are products of your creative mind:

_____

_____

_____

Like Claire, you may have come to similar conclusions about the significance you've placed on your distressing intrusive thoughts. You realize you've been treating them like an emotional catastrophe.

Now it's time to generate a more realistic, balanced interpretation based on the work you've done in these exercises. This last step involves developing a detoxified interpretation of the distressing thought.

Detoxifying Your Interpretation

Coming up with an alternative interpretation or narrative that emphasizes more realistic, benign, and normal aspects of the negative intrusion can be difficult, especially if you've been treating the intrusion as a highly significant threat for years and years. You'll want to base this narrative on the work you've done in the previous exercises. You may want to review the old interpretation of emotional significance that you generated for the mental-control profile in chapter 3 and consider how to revise this interpretation so it's a nontoxic explanation.

You may find it helpful to have a look at the detoxification narrative that Claire wrote. Notice how it is a more realistic, balanced interpretation of her distressing intrusion.

It's perfectly normal to have negative intrusive thoughts about surgery. How could anyone who is facing major surgery not think about it? I can use the intrusive thought as a reminder that I'm dealing with my health problem in the most constructive way possible. I can think about all the practical things I need to do to prepare for the surgery and the long post-operative recovery period. Whether I have these intrusive thoughts or not makes no difference to the outcome of the operation or to my quality of life after. In reality, this surgery is not the most difficult thing I've faced in my life, and certainly a number of my friends have had to deal with more dire health concerns, such as recurrence of cancer. Rather than trying to inhibit the surgery intrusions, I'll welcome them in my mind as spontaneous reminders that I'm taking good care of my health.

Notice that Claire didn't reinterpret her thoughts about the unwanted surgery as meaningless. Sometimes our mental intrusions really are truly meaningless, but other times they are intrinsically more significant, and so you have to turn them into positive aspects of your mental life. Claire decided to treat the intrusions as positive, self-affirming reminders. This could also be the best reinterpretation strategy for your distressing intrusion. Whether you reinterpret the thought as meaningless or as a positive indicator, however, it's important to generate a reinterpretation that strips it of emotional significance.

EXERCISE: Write a Detoxification Narrative

Follow these suggestions and guidelines to reinterpret your distressing intrusion:

Your reinterpretation should emphasize how the intrusion is more neutral and less negative and threatening than you've been assuming.

The narrative should be a reappraisal of the intrusion, emphasizing evidence from your own experience that it's okay to consider it a normal mental intrusion of minimal significance.

Think of the intrusion as a product of your imagination with no direct connection to your real-life experience. Just having the thought pop into your mind can't by itself cause terrible things to happen to you or to your loved ones.

Notice how it's possible to experience the intrusive thought without letting it impact your everyday life.

Since you have no choice on whether the intrusion pops into your mind, can you turn the experience into something positive that affirms your personal integrity and value? For example, the intrusion could be considered a sign that you are creative or that you're a sensitive and caring person or that you have high moral standards.

Make sure that your nontoxic, normalized narrative is consistent with your real-life experience of the intrusion. You'll have a hard time convincing yourself of any interpretation that isn't plausible.

Now, with these considerations in mind, write your reinterpretation in the space provided. Then compare your narrative with the interpretation of insignificance that you generated for your nontoxic negative thought. The two narratives should be quite similar. If not, consider how you can revise the reinterpretation of your toxic intrusion so that it is less significant and threatening.

_____

_____

_____

_____

_____

_____

Have you been able to construct a detoxified explanation for your distressing intrusive thought, image, or memory that minimizes its emotional significance and importance? If you're still struggling with detoxification after all this work, don't give up. Mental detoxification is one of the most important intervention skills taught in the workbook.

Once you have a nontoxic perspective on the distressing intrusion, you'll find the workbook's control strategies to be more effective. Don't worry if you're not yet able to put your nontoxic interpretation into practice. Greater belief and acceptance of this reinterpretation will come with time and effort. To help with this process, use the self-help exercises presented in this final section.

Practicing Detoxification

Now that you've developed a healthier, more realistic perspective on your distressing intrusive thought, it's important to put it into practice. The only way to use this detoxification intervention to reduce your anxiety or depression is to practice catching the distressing intrusion and then responding to it with a reinterpretation of the thought. Doing some reality testing in your daily life is a great way to start doing this.

Reality Testing

Reality testing involves looking for evidence that confirms your reinterpretation of the intrusion as a benign occurrence with minimal emotional significance. This means that whenever you're aware of the toxic intrusion, you take a minute to look around and gather evidence that supports a reinterpretation of the intrusion's significance.

Imagine, for example, you're flying and suddenly have the distressing thought *What if the plane crashes?* You can feel a jolt of anxiety pierce your body. Obviously, your automatic interpretation is *I'm in danger of dying in a horrible crash.* So you look around and note that everyone else is calm, the airline stewards are going about their work in a friendly and serene manner, and there has been no change in how the plane functions. Clearly the objective external evidence supports a reinterpretation of what's happening, which is *I'm having an imaginative negative intrusive thought; I'm not in any more danger now than I was a few minutes ago. Clearly my thinking is completely disconnected and irrelevant to what is happening around me.* In this case, you are using reality testing to support the reinterpretation; that is, you're noting that despite what's happening in your head, the external data indicates there has been no change in your level of danger. The thought of crashing is a product of your imagination, albeit a highly unpleasant bit of imaginative thinking.

It's important to record any evidence that confirms your reinterpretation of the distressing intrusion. Whenever you have an experience that reminds you that the intrusion is benign, you can make note of it, perhaps in your Smartphone, and then transfer this information into the workbook using the space in the next exercise. This will become a list of evidence that the distressing thought is not a significant personal threat; you'll be able to review this list whenever you get stuck on exaggerating the significance of the distressing intrusion.

EXERCISE: Capture the Moment

List evidence that you've collected from your moment-by-moment experience to show that the distressing intrusive thought is not a significant personal threat.

1. _____

2. _____

3. _____

4. _____

5. _____

Did you discover that the reality was different from what you imagined would happen? Reality testing can help strengthen your belief that your distress is more a product of intrusive thinking than a product of the current situation.

Obviously there are times when our circumstances are upsetting. But reality testing helps you develop a more balanced perspective on your situation as you practice catching your exaggerated interpretations of emotional significance. You are using more objective data from your daily life to arrive at a realistic, neutral interpretation that detoxifies your unwanted intrusive thoughts and feelings.

Exposure-Based Detoxification

Another great way to practice your new understanding of the toxic intrusion is to schedule time to intentionally focus on the thought. This therapeutic strategy is based on *imaginal exposure*, an effective intervention for worry (Borkovec et al. 1983). In this procedure, you set aside time to intentionally and repeatedly think about your worries. You schedule at least thirty minutes each day to sit and intentionally bring all your worries to mind and think intently on them. When you do this, the distressing quality of the worry declines over time because you feel more in control of the worry, gain new insights into the worry, or simply become bored with the worry topic.

You can use this strategy to practice detoxifying your distressing intrusive thought.

EXERCISE: Schedule Imagined Exposure

Start by planning a daily thirty-minute exposure session, choosing a location where you'll be comfortable and free from distractions. Make sure you have with you the description of the toxic intrusive thought and the detoxified interpretation that you completed earlier in this chapter.

1. Take the first two to three minutes to feel physically relaxed. You can do this by focusing on your breath and paying attention to the experience of taking slow but full diaphragmatic breaths.

2. Next bring to mind the distressing intrusive thought. You should try to experience the intrusion as fully as possible, reflecting on its various characteristics and implications.

3. Once the distressing thought is fully in your mind, thoughtfully read aloud the detoxified interpretation. Reflect on the various arguments you made for considering the intrusion a normal spontaneous thought with diminished significance. Focus on the normality of the intrusion, its imaginative elements, and the minimal consequences to your everyday experience. Think about your neutral reinterpretation of the intrusion as deeply as possible.

4. After spending approximately five minutes on the nontoxic interpretation, return to a focus on the breath, taking a couple of minutes to relax your body.

5. Repeat steps 2 and 3 several times throughout the thirty-minute exposure session.

6. Expect your mind to wander. When you are distracted by other thoughts, acknowledge the distraction and then gently bring your attention back to the intrusion and its reinterpretation.

Imagined exposure can be a very effective procedure for stripping distressing thoughts of their meaning, strengthening your belief in your reinterpretation, and, as a result, reducing the anxiety, depression, or other negative emotions associated with these thoughts.

You'll want to practice this intervention on a daily basis for at least two weeks. If you've not been able to detoxify the intrusion in that time period, you may need to continue with exposure sessions longer. Also, it's possible you've not quite generated a credible insignificance interpretation, so you may need to spend more time revising your detoxification narrative.

Wrap-Up

The meaning we attach to the thoughts, memories, and ideas that suddenly pop into our mind determines how they make us feel. If you suddenly have a thought you consider brilliant, pleasant, or exciting, you'll feel great. But if you have an intrusive thought that you consider threatening, highly negative, or discouraging, you'll feel anxious, depressed, or guilty, or experience other negative emotions. This chapter focused on the meanings or interpretations that can turn your intrusive thoughts into highly distressing, toxic mental events. It emphasized how to correct the meaning attached to distressing thoughts to give them less emotional impact. Learning to reinterpret distressing intrusive thoughts includes

- Discovering how you interpret particular intrusive thoughts, images, or memories in a highly significant manner, so they become toxic mental experiences.

- Realizing you have negative intrusive thoughts that are not distressing, because they are considered insignificant or meaningless. However, these nontoxic intrusions have the potential to become highly distressing if they are misinterpreted.

- Constructing a reinterpretation of your toxic mental intrusions to make them normal and benign or even insignificant. This is the most important step in detoxifying your distressing thoughts and feelings.

- Accepting the more benign or neutral meaning of your distressing intrusion, as evidence from real-life supports your detoxified interpretation, and repeated, intentional exposure to the intrusion reduces its impact.

Changing beliefs is an extraordinarily difficult task. Most of us adopt a certain perspective and find it almost impossible to see things another way. Don't be surprised if you found the approach in this chapter difficult to use at first. It may take time and patience to understand your unwanted distressing intrusive thoughts in a more neutral manner. You should also feel encouraged, though, as you've discovered that you already interpret many of your negative intrusive thoughts in a healthy way. The challenge is to recognize this natural tendency to attribute insignificance to many of your negative intrusions and respond similarly when you have a toxic intrusive thought. No doubt you've made a good start in this direction. Now it's time to build on this learning and focus on the second major contributor to anxiety or depression: the adverse effects of the mental-control paradox.

CHAPTER 5

Control Skills: Letting Go

Giving up on a struggle can be a difficult choice. It could be a stressful situation in which stepping back from the problem would be best, but you're afraid to let go. Maybe it's a longstanding relationship conflict, a difficult work environment, or a chronic health problem. Letting go of control can be hard, and yet in some situations, acceptance will lead to the better outcome. Take, for example, an incident that happened to me several years ago. While swimming, I suddenly found myself caught in strong current that was sweeping me further from shore. I became panicky when I realized I couldn't swim against the current. After several minutes of futile swimming and encroaching physical exhaustion, however, I took a chance and stopped struggling long enough to discover that I could just barely touch bottom. I was actually safe but only discovered this when I stopped trying to swim against the current.

EXERCISE: When Have You Let Go?

Have you had experiences in your life where you discovered that relinquishing control and accepting a particular situation was the best option? Take a few minutes to recall some of these experiences and list a couple in the space provided.

_____

_____

_____

_____

_____

You'll be reminded of these experiences later in the chapter.

Letting go of ineffective mental-control strategies is the focus of this chapter. From chapter 4, you've learned how to reduce the personal significance of your toxic mental intrusions, but before you can adopt more effective mental-control strategies, you need to understand the limits of self-control and reduce your reliance on mental-control strategies that aren't working. This chapter builds on what you learned in chapter 2 about the paradox of mental control, examining the unique problems associated with self-control of unwanted thoughts and feelings. It introduces the concept of *trying too hard*; that is, when you're putting too much effort into controlling unwanted thoughts. It will also talk about two barriers to letting go of self-control: a tendency to overthink and a tendency to hold erroneous assumptions about mental control.

As you work through this chapter, you will want to remind yourself of other times when letting go of control in difficult situations did help you cope with life's problems. You can return to the previous exercise to review what you recorded. This same approach can be applied to your unwanted distressing thoughts and feelings. To begin, it will help to examine Leah's problems with mental self-control.

Leah's Story: Haunted by Regrets

Leah struggled with self-doubt and regret. After twenty years in a marriage that once had been a fairy tale romance, she decided to leave. As a highly successful forty-four-year-old realtor and mother, Leah had accomplished much but felt trapped in a dying and loveless marriage. The initial separation was followed by a long litigation battle over child custody and spousal support payments. But after three years, Leah prevailed, and she settled into her new life as a working single mother. At first, she felt a renewed self-confidence and freedom, but as the months passed, Leah found herself feeling more and more depressed.

Leah was hopeful she'd rediscover love after the divorce. As an attractive, sociable, and extroverted young adult, she'd had many romantic relationships, so hope burned strong that she'd find her true soul mate. But the dating scene had changed dramatically since her youth, and Leah was having difficulty connecting with men her age. As time passed, Leah became more and more convinced she'd never find true love. The future looked bleak and lonely. When feeling down, Leah started having intrusive thoughts of regret. Over and over in her mind, she could hear these words: *I've made a terrible mistake. I was better off when I was married. How could I have been so stupid? I don't have what it takes to be loved.*

The intrusions of regret started a cycle of negative, self-critical thinking that caused Leah to feel a depth of despair that at times frightened her. She realized the regretful intrusions were toxic, but no matter how hard she tried, she seemed powerless to control them. She tried pushing the thoughts from her mind, reassuring herself that she was better off than so many others or reminding herself of times when her husband was mean and uncaring. But nothing helped. Despite her strongest efforts at self-control, nothing stopped the relentless intrusions from within.

Like Leah, you may be feeling discouraged by your efforts to control distressing intrusive thoughts. No matter how hard you try to change your way of thinking, you find the intrusions returning and, along with them, an overwhelming distress. Leah was determined to get a better grip on her life, so she spent long hours trying to analyze her feelings and understand her descent into self-pity. But Leah was taking the wrong approach to her distressing thoughts and feelings. She had never learned the art of letting go, and now one of her greatest barriers to progress was a tendency to overthink things.

Too Much in Your Head

Are you a deep thinker? Are you keenly aware of your thoughts, often analyzing the causes and consequences of what you are thinking? If so, you could be prone to *overthinking*, or spending too much time in your own head. Overthinking refers to an excessive tendency to monitor, evaluate, and control all types of thinking (Janeck et al. 2003). Of course, our survival depends on being aware of our thoughts, a capacity to evaluate them, and an ability to direct our thought processes so we can reach important life goals. But overthinking takes this natural feature of human thinking too far. Overthinkers tend to be highly introspective and excessively concerned with controlling their thoughts and feelings. Because of this inward focus, overthinking complicates efforts to deal with negative states like obsessive thinking, worry, and rumination (Cartwright-Hatton and Wells 1997).

Overthinkers often put too much effort into controlling their unwanted thoughts, so they easily fall victim to the paradox of mental control, where more effort equals less control. Overthinking can also contribute to a fear of losing control. You may be wondering if you are an overthinker. The next exercise will help you determine if you have a tendency to overthink.

EXERCISE: The Overthinking Test

Read each statement and check the ones that apply to you. If you're unsure, you could ask a spouse, close friend, or family member for their opinion.

_____ *I can easily become aware of my thoughts at any moment.*

_____ *I have a good understanding of how my mind works.*

_____ *I often question or evaluate my thoughts.*

_____ *I often focus on changing the way I think about situations, other people, or myself.*

_____ *I'm keenly aware of becoming upset by unwanted thoughts.*

_____ *I can be easily distracted by my thinking.*

_____ *I often monitor what I am thinking.*

_____ *It's important that I maintain control over unwanted and distressing thoughts.*

_____ *I'm a highly intuitive, self-aware individual.*

_____ *I'm a deep thinker.*

_____ *I'm a detailed person who has difficulty just sitting with a problem.*

_____ *I tend to search for the deeper meaning in everything.*

_____ *I have a strong need to know, to understand.*

_____ *I have difficulty tolerating uncertainty, ambiguity, and lack of clarity.*

The more statements you checked as applicable, the greater the likelihood that overthinking is hindering your control of negative emotion. If you endorsed seven or more statements, you may very well be spending too much time in your head.

Leah often fell into the overthinking trap. When intrusions of regret flooded her mind, she'd get caught in an endless cycle of analyzing their truthfulness, because she wanted to think more positively. She had trouble getting to sleep at night because of racing thoughts and so searched for a solution to achieve some control over what she called her "runaway mind."

Although Leah's insight and intuitiveness served her well when dealing with interpersonal problems, her heightened self-awareness was a liability when it came to unwanted thoughts about the divorce. So to deal more effectively with runaway thinking, Leah began catching herself when she slipped into overthinking. This helped her realize she was trying too hard to control her thoughts and needed to let go of her need to control.

If you've come to the conclusion that you often fall prey to overthinking, like Leah you'll want to work on spending less time in your head. The next exercise can help you begin to reduce this problematic thinking style. It's intended to help you do two things: be more aware of the negative effects of overthinking and practice catching times when you slip into an overthinking style. You might say to yourself, *There I go again. I'm getting trapped by overthinking. This isn't helpful.*

EXERCISE: Overthinking Awareness

Review the mental-intrusion diary in chapter 3. You should be using this diary on a regular basis to capture your unwanted distressing intrusions. Reread each entry, and in the response column, write the letters OT if you notice that you had slipped into overthinking when you responded to the intrusion. Remember, overthinking refers to spending an excessive amount of time trying to analyze the causes and consequences of your distressing thoughts and feelings.

Now that you've marked your mental-intrusion diary for instances of overthinking, how often did you slip into this unhelpful way of responding to your distress? Did the overthinking have a negative effect on your unwanted thoughts and feelings? In some instances, did it seem helpful? You won't be motivated to change this coping strategy unless you are convinced that overthinking has a negative effect on your emotions.

If you still believe that thinking deeply about your intrusive thoughts is important, you'll need to spend extra time in the next section, which deals with unhelpful beliefs about the need and importance of mental control. Another strategy to counter overthinking is to practice taking a more relaxed approach to mental control by allowing yourself periods of mind wandering and daydreaming (see chapter 6 for further discussion). This involves accepting whatever thoughts pop into your mind without evaluation, manipulation, or control.

Regardless of how often you slip into the overthinking mode, letting go of excessive mental control will reduce your personal distress. But letting go will be impossible if you believe in the importance of strict mental control. The next section talks about two core beliefs that could be reinforcing your investment in mental control.

Debunking Mental-Control Myths

Again, trying hard to directly inhibit distressing intrusive thoughts often makes matters worse. The harder we work at self-control, the more persistent our negative thoughts and feelings are. When this happens, it is understandable that we will intensify our effort, becoming even more convinced of the importance of strict self-control. For example, as Leah's thoughts of regret became more and more uncontrollable, she only intensified her efforts to suppress these thoughts. This is because she failed to understand the paradox of mental control: that the harder you try, the less controllable the unwanted thought is. If you can relate to this situation—if doubling down on control still seems like the answer—taking a closer look at your beliefs about mental control could be beneficial. There are two beliefs, in particular, that could stifle your use of effective strategies to reduce anxiety and depression, so it's important to debunk these mental-control myths.

Belief Myth: More Control Is the Answer

Possibly you've concluded that more mental-control effort is necessary to deal with distressing thoughts, because you believe you're calmer and less distressed when you're in complete control. No doubt there are times when you're in a positive mood and you also feel a strong sense of self-control. However, many variables influence our mood. And while a heightened sense of self-control certainly contributes to overall life satisfaction and well-being, the influence that our mental-control effort has over momentary mood changes may be less than we think. Could you be giving too much weight to the contribution of strong mental control in creating a positive mood?

Leah, for example, noticed that often her mood improved when she shifted her thoughts from the past and focused on a current work task. However, sometimes she just felt good for no apparent reason or without conscious effort to feel better. And there were other times when efforts to focus on the moment or think more positively utterly failed. What Leah learned from these experiences is that mental control has a more precarious impact on mood than she had assumed. More mental control was not always the answer for mood repair.

If you're like most people, you've probably never examined whether making a greater mental-control effort actually produces a better mood state. Often the beliefs we hold about our thoughts and feelings are assumptions that we've adopted serendipitously. However, given the negative effects of the mental-control paradox, it's important to have an accurate understanding of the connection between mental-control effort and mood. The next exercise is designed to help you carry out an investigation to determine whether you might be overstating the influence of your mental-control effort on your daily mood.

EXERCISE: Mood-and-Control Record

Over the next week, take note of times of significant positive or negative mood. In the column on the left, indicate whether it was a positive mood or a negative mood, and rate its intensity. In the column on the right, rate the extent that your mood was due to a conscious effort to suppress, inhibit, or direct attention away from your thoughts. If you need more space, visit http://www.newharbinger.com/38426 to download other copies of this mood-and-control record.

Mood-and-Control Record

Mood State (Label whether mood positive or negative; rate mood intensity from 1 = mild, 2 = moderate, 3 = strong.)	Rate Mental-Control Effort (0 = no effort, 1 = slight effort, 2 = moderate effort, 3 = strong effort)
1.	
2.	
3.	
4.	
5.	
6.	
7.	
8.	
9.	
10.	

If you kept a mood-and-control record over the last week, congratulations! Rarely do we systematically test our beliefs about the mind. Instead, we tend to assume we know what affects our thoughts and feelings.

So what did you learn about the effects of mental-control effort on your mood fluctuations? Respond to these questions:

1. What's the relationship between your mood state and how much you try to control your thoughts? Did you only feel good when your mental-control effort was high and worse when mental-control effort was low?

    _____

2. How effective were you at changing your mood state by exerting greater mental-control effort?

    _____

3. Did a calm or positive mood ever happen without conscious effort on your part?

    _____

4. Did you have spontaneous positive thoughts or daydreams that made you feel good without any effort on your part?

    _____

    _____

5. How often did you feel like you had strong mental or emotional control without much conscious effort on your part?

    _____

    _____

Intuitively, we all believe that more self-control is better. But greater control effort is not always the answer to better mood. Recall the life experiences you noted at the beginning of this chapter. Often, greater control effort is associated with more distress, whereas letting go of mental-control effort can have beneficial effects on your mood state.

Belief Myth: Maybe You Will "Snap"

Another common belief that could be keeping you hooked into trying to control your thoughts is the fear that if you don't control them, you will lose complete control or even "snap" and do something irrational (see chapter 2). Is this one of your basic fears? Leah had a strong fear of losing control. She firmly believed that she couldn't let the intrusive thoughts of regret take over, because they'd cause her to slip further into a depressive funk. So Leah fought hard against these thoughts, fearful she was losing her grip. If, like Leah, you believe that easing up on your mental-control efforts might push you toward a complete loss of control, then letting go of control will seem particularly frightening. You might question if taking a more relaxed approach to self-control could lead to some type of mental catastrophe. Maybe you've actually asked yourself, *Could I snap?* For you, the catastrophe might be experiencing runaway thoughts or intense emotional distress or taking impulsive actions that could harm yourself or others. Whatever the imagined catastrophe, the basic fear is that letting go could make matters much worse.

Like before, it's important to evaluate the accuracy of your belief by collecting data from your daily experiences. You can take an evidence-based approach to determine how close you've come to losing complete control over your thoughts, feelings, or behavior. The next exercise asks you to recall unpleasant past experiences of losing self-control. It could be loss of control over thoughts, feelings, or behavior, which left you feeling that self-control was in short supply.

EXERCISE: Memories of Lost Control

On a blank sheet of paper, make a list of past experiences in which you seriously lost control over your thoughts, feelings, or behavior. These would include times when you caused unintended and significant inconvenience, to yourself or others. Based on these experiences, answer each of the following questions:

1. How often did you *actually* lose complete control, and how often was the experience more like a *feeling* that you were out of control?

    _____

    _____

2. Were there ways that you exercised some control in these situations, but these responses were overshadowed by the ways that you exercised poor self-control?

_____

_____

3. Is it more accurate to describe these experiences as times of low self-control or as times of complete absence of control?

_____

_____

4. Did others think you were out of control?

_____

_____

5. Looking back, were the consequences of having low self-control as devastating as you assumed they would be at the time?

_____

_____

As you review your worst memories of losing control, do you think your fears of losing complete control are justified? Would it be more accurate to describe your worst experiences as times of low self-control rather than complete loss of control? Even during times of serious anger outbursts or impulsivity, people normally continue to exhibit some degree of directed action and restraint. Do you agree that it's more accurate to remember these experiences as times when you should have exercised more control over what you said, how you felt, or how you behaved? You can use the findings from this exercise to challenge your fear of losing complete control. If the problem you face is low self-control rather than complete loss of control, then easing up on mental-control effort at appropriate times will not lead to the disastrous outcome you fear.

At this point, let me offer a caveat. Sometimes exercising poor self-control can lead to grievous harm both for oneself and others. Humanity is full of rage, anger, and hostility, which has caused much misery in the lives of hundreds of millions worldwide. Note that the focus of this workbook is on how fear of losing control and its associated tendency of overcontrol contribute to anxiety, depression, obsessionality, and other negative emotions. If the major problem in your life is poor self-control, impulsivity, or emotion dysregulation, you should consider a different workbook that deals with these issues more directly. You'll find some recommended self-help materials in the resource section. If a loss of control over feelings and behavior has caused serious problems in your personal life, then you may also want to consider reaching out to a qualified psychiatrist, psychologist, social worker, or other mental health professional.

Leah struggled with difficulty controlling her intrusive thoughts of regret, but she also discovered from the previous exercises that greater mental control was not the cure for her depressed mood or fears. Ironically, she actually had a reputation for being quite calm and controlled under stress. Despite her personal battle with the intrusive thoughts of regret, Leah learned that she was generally a well-controlled person. She didn't need to try harder to practice self-control. Leah needed a different approach to deal with her thoughts of regret. But before she could let go of control, it was also important for her to evaluate whether her responses to her mental intrusions, that is, her actual control strategies, might have unintended negative effects on unwanted thoughts and feelings.

By now, you too may be realizing that your issues with mental control are more nuanced than you first realized. You may see that you get trapped in overthinking sometimes; you may also recognize that you hold erroneous beliefs about your level of self-control. Now it's time to examine the third major feature of mental self-control: the actual strategies you use to control distressing intrusions.

Weak Control Strategies

We all have a tendency to seize on the most immediate control strategy when feeling emotionally upset. We can't just stand idly by and do nothing when faced with distressing intrusive thoughts (Freeston et al. 1995; Purdon and Clark 1994). Unfortunately, our first control response is often our least effective strategy. The next exercise includes a list of five common mental-control strategies that you may use when you are upset.

EXERCISE: Weak-Strategies Checklist

Consider each strategy and place a checkmark (√) beside any that you tend to use when responding to unwanted intrusive thoughts and feelings. You might find it helpful to consult your responses to the mental-control strategies questionnaire in chapter 3.

Control Strategy	Explanation	Example
_____ Unfocused distraction	Using multiple, unrelated distractors to draw attention away from a recurring intrusive thought	When the thoughts of regret intruded, Leah tried to think about her work, supper plans, the weather, news events, anything to draw her attention toward something else.
_____ Self-criticism	Making self-critical, disparaging comments for having the intrusion	Leah would feel frustrated when the intrusions returned and would tell herself to stop being so selfish and pitiful.
_____ Neutralization/ compulsive rituals	Responding in ways to try to counter or cancel the distress or negative effects of an intrusive thought	When she felt guilt and negativity over her decision to leave the marriage, Leah would sometimes try to recall a good decision she made.
_____ Reassurance seeking	Seeking information from others or external sources to reduce your concern about the unacceptability or feared consequences of the intrusion	Leah would sometimes consult with her closest friends about whether she had made the right decision to divorce.
_____ Rationalizations	Reasoning with yourself that everything will be all right	When regretful thoughts popped into her mind, Leah tried to convince herself that she'd made the right decision.

Which strategies did you end up checking? It's likely these are your most immediate responses when feeling upset. These control strategies are among the least effective in dealing with unwanted thoughts.

Most of us tend to overuse these strategies when feeling emotionally distressed or overwhelmed (Wegner and Pennebaker 1993). But the checklist is based on your impression of your mental-control strategies. You will need to look more closely at each strategy to see how well it's working for you. The first of these strategies is unfocused distraction, which is probably the most common response to distressing intrusive thoughts.

Unfocused Distraction

When we have distressing intrusive thoughts, we may naturally try to distract ourselves by switching our attention to some other topic or idea. However, when using distraction in this way, our natural tendency is to use an *unfocused* strategy. For example, when Leah had intrusive thoughts of regret, she tried to refocus her attention on work, her son, the evening meal, a planned weekend activity with a friend, and the like, in an effort to keep out the intrusive thought.

When she had the intrusive thought *I should never have left the marriage*, she immediately tried to think of something else, such as what she'd have for supper that evening. Unfortunately, the unwanted thought returned fairly quickly, so Leah tried to think of something else, such as what her son was doing at that moment in school. Once again, the distraction was effective only momentarily, and when it returned, Leah tried to think about her weekend. Over a very few minutes, Leah might jump from one topic to the next in her effort to suppress intrusive thoughts of regret.

Harvard psychologist Daniel Wegner (2011) calls this *unfocused distraction* and shows that it is an ineffective way to control unwanted intrusive thoughts. Wegner argues that the use of multiple distractors is a weak mental-control strategy because the distressing intrusion becomes associated with many ongoing thoughts and feeling states, so multiple distractors now act as a trigger for the intrusion. In Leah's case, supper, her son at school, and plans for the weekend became reminders of the intrusive thoughts of regret because she always tried to use them as distractors. Rather than diverting attention away from the intrusion, they became cues to remind her of the unwanted thought.

Another problem is that when anxious or depressed, we tend to select negative distractors because they are consistent with our mood state (Conway, Howell, and Giannopoulas 1991). When Leah had bouts of depressed mood, she'd respond to intrusions of regret by thinking about all the problems in her life or all her personal faults. These negative distractors were even more powerful reminders of the intrusion because they matched its emotional tone. Thus this spontaneous self-distraction strategy becomes a weak approach to controlling distressing thoughts.

How often do you slip into unfocused distraction when struggling with a negative mood state? The next exercise is a great way to determine how much you use unfocused distraction, and it provides a test of the utility of this heightened mental-control effort. Called the *alternate-days experiment*, it was first proposed for obsessive thinking (Rachman 2003).

EXERCISE: The Alternative-Days Experiment

Plan to conduct the alternate-days experiment over a two-week period. Start by dividing your week into high mental-control and low mental-control days. For example, you could select Monday, Wednesday, Friday, and Sunday as low-control days and Tuesday, Thursday, and Saturday as high-control days. During low-control days, devote as little attention as possible to consciously controlling your emotional thoughts and affect. During these days, allow yourself to think or feel whatever comes into your mind without consciously trying to control what you are thinking or feeling. That is, let go of your mental-control effort. Then on high-control days, work on paying close attention to your emotional thoughts, and try hard to inhibit any unwanted negative intrusive thoughts and feelings. In particular, try to distract yourself with many different ideas, thoughts, and memories, letting your mind flit from one topic to the next.

Use the next set of questions to reflect on the most important aspects of your mental-control experience. Record your responses at the end of the day in the worksheet that follows, so you can compare the effectiveness of unfocused distraction during high-control days versus the effectiveness of letting go of control on low-control days. You can also visit http://www.newharbinger.com/38426 to download other copies of the high mental control vs. letting go of mental control worksheet.

1. Was using unfocused distraction on high-control days more, less, or equally effective to letting go of control on low-control days? Did you have more, fewer, or an equal number of distressing thoughts and feelings on the different days?

2. Was using unfocused distraction on high-control days more stressful or frustrating than taking a more relaxed approach to mental control?

3. Was your emotional state any better on high-control days than on low-control days, or was it worse? How much better or worse? If there was little difference, is greater effort at control worth it?

4. Can you think of any other advantages or disadvantages to using unfocused distraction on high-control days?

High Mental Control vs. Letting Go of Mental Control Worksheet

Days	Effectiveness of High Mental-Control Effort	Effectiveness of Low Mental-Control Effort
Monday		
Tuesday		
Wednesday		
Thursday		
Friday		
Saturday		
Sunday		

Did you notice any benefits to exerting greater mental control, or were the days of low mental control any better? The alternate-days experiment may seem tedious, but I hope you found it helpful in highlighting the negative effects of unfocused distraction and an excessive mental-control effort.

Many people actually feel better during low-control days, whereas others come to realize that a greater control effort is not worth it; that the difference between high-control days and low-control days is so negligible that it's just not worth the effort. Whatever your experience, the critical question is whether trying hard to control your intrusive thoughts is more harmful than helpful.

As mentioned, when you use unfocused distraction to inhibit an unwanted intrusion, the distractors can actually become reminders of the unwanted intrusion. If this is happening to you, you can counter these effects by using a more effective focused-distraction strategy discussed in chapter 7.

Other Weak Control Strategies

Four other mental-control responses listed in the weak-strategies checklist can have a deleterious effect on unwanted thoughts and feelings: these are self-criticism, neutralization or compulsive rituals, reassurance seeking, and rationalization.

SELF-CRITICISM

Are you prone to self-criticism, especially when feeling down or discouraged? Self-criticism is a natural response if you've been unsuccessful in bringing distressing thoughts and feelings under control. One can easily end up making self-disparaging remarks such as *I'm being so weak* or *pitiful* or *lazy* or *pathetic*. You may be hoping that verbal self-punishment will motivate you to have better control over your distress. In reality, this practically never works. In fact, self-criticism is highly ineffective and only intensifies negative emotional states like depression (Halvorsen et al. 2015). This type of response is often so automatic that it can be hard to detect. We can slip into a fresh round of self-deprecation before we even know it. You need to watch out for elevations in self-criticism.

NEUTRALIZATION OR COMPULSIVE RITUALS

Neutralization or compulsive rituals can develop when the same distressing intrusive thought keeps returning over and over again. The best example of neutralization strategies can be seen in OCD: a person who fears she has become contaminated by touching a dirty object, such as a doorknob, may compulsively wash her hands in order to eliminate (that is, neutralize) the possibility of contamination, thereby restoring a sense of safety and relief. Although most common in OCD, neutralization can occur in other states that involve repetitive distressing thoughts (Bjornsson and Phillips 2014).

To try to cancel out, or neutralize, the negative effects of her intrusive thoughts of regret, Leah would form a clear image in her mind of important positive life events, such as the day she decided which university to attend, her decision to accept various job offers, the day she discovered she was pregnant, or the birth of her son. Leah was hoping that vividly reliving these past positive experiences would counter the distress and negativity felt over the divorce. However, neutralization actually makes obsessive thinking worse by increasing the intensity and importance of the unwanted thought (Clark 2004). So it's important to determine whether you commonly use neutralization or compulsive rituals in response to recurring negative intrusions.

REASSURANCE SEEKING

How often have you been worried about something and turned to your spouse, family member, or friend, and said, "How do you think it will go?" Maybe you've discovered a skin rash, you're concerned about possible melanoma, and so you've scheduled an appointment with your family doctor. But as you wait for the appointment, you become more anxious and worried about the possible diagnosis. And so you find yourself asking others, "Do you think I'll be okay? Do you think it's only a benign skin rash?" Of course, you're looking for others to say it will be fine. And when you hear those words, "It will be fine. It's probably nothing," it's like magic. You feel a sudden, but brief, sense of relief. It's as if hearing the reassurance over and over somehow makes it more likely that you'll hear good news from your doctor.

Such reassurance seeking is another maladaptive mental-control response to unwanted thoughts and feelings. There are two major problems with it. First, reassurance seeking is ineffective in relieving distress or reducing unwanted intrusive thoughts. And second, it may actually intensify unwanted negative thoughts and feelings (Salkovskis and Kobori 2015). The reason is that reassurance seeking is a type of magical or superstitious thinking. For it to work, you have to pretend that the person giving the reassurance knows the future. If you're asking a friend for reassurance about a medical test, you have to pretend that she has expert knowledge of the disease and that she can predict the future. Naturally, both of these preconditions are absurd, and so reassurance seeking simply becomes a self-imposed mind game. Learning to kick the reassurance-seeking habit is an important step toward letting go of excessive mental-control efforts.

RATIONALIZATION

When distressed by intrusive thoughts, you may try to convince yourself with the rationalization that *Everything will be all right* or *Don't worry, it's going to be okay*; that any negative consequence associated with the intrusion won't happen. It's a type of self-reassurance that doesn't work, because such vague, uncertain platitudes may be temporarily comforting but are hardly convincing. For example, Leah would say to herself *I'll be fine; everything will turn out fine*, but she really couldn't see how her future looked any brighter, so telling herself this did little to squelch her distressing thoughts and feelings of regret. In the end, rationalization is ineffective in dealing with the negative thoughts that fuel a deep-seated uncertainty about the future.

The final exercise in this chapter is useful for increasing your sense of when you may be using any of these four ineffective control strategies.

EXERCISE: Weak-Control Awareness

Go back to the entries you've made in your mental-intrusion diary over the past couple of weeks. Review the information you recorded to determine whether any of your responses to distress could be considered a maladaptive control strategy. You can use initials to identify each strategy such as SC for self-criticism, NC for neutralization or compulsive ritual, RS for reassurance seeking, and RA for rationalization. If you don't have sufficient information in your mental-intrusion diary to do this exercise, keep track of your intrusions over the next week or two, paying close attention to your response to the distress and whether you were relying on any of the maladaptive strategies.

Are certain maladaptive control strategies particularly problematic for you? If so, the frustration you feel over poor control of intrusive thoughts and feelings may be due to reliance on these ineffective strategies.

Leah came to the realization that the solution to her distress was to stop trying so hard to control her thoughts and feelings, and instead to let go of control. This was a refreshing perspective for her. Instead of blaming herself for poor control, she began to see that her problem was more strategic in nature. With this insight, she gained renewed hope that her life could get better if she adopted a new approach to unwanted thoughts and feelings.

Now that you're more aware of your own natural responses to mental intrusions and the strategies you use, the next step is to learn more effective ways to deal with your distressing intrusive thoughts and feelings.

Wrap-Up

Common sense tells us to try harder when we seem to be failing. And yet, when it comes to distressing intrusive thoughts and feelings, trying harder sometimes ends up causing more rather than less distress. The truth is that just the opposite approach is needed for unwanted intrusions. Instead of buckling down on control, it is the willingness to let go that is most critical. Indeed, letting go is often the best option for many of life's most intractable problems. However, it's easier said than done, and so this chapter highlighted many factors that can stand in your way:

- Excessive awareness and analysis of your unwanted thoughts and feelings leads to a greater investment in efforts to control them. Learning to recognize when you are overthinking is an important skill.

- Holding on to misconceptions about the benefits of using strong mental-control effort against intrusions is a barrier to letting go of control.

- Often the mental-control strategies that feel most natural, like unfocused distraction, reassurance seeking, and rationalization, are the least effective in reducing unwanted intrusive thoughts, images, and memories.

The work you did in this chapter has helped you become more aware of your coping strategies as well as any misguided beliefs that may be getting in the way of positive personal change. This increased awareness is an important step in transforming your approach to distressing intrusive thoughts and feelings. You now know whether your self-help therapy should target overthinking, faulty beliefs about mental control, or a reliance on ineffective control strategies. Like Leah, the problem is not you but rather your approach to mental intrusions. It's a problem of strategy not biology. However, changing our mindful ways is not easy. To be successful, an attitude of self-acceptance and compassion is needed, which is the topic of the next chapter.

CHAPTER 6

Control Skills: Mindful Self-Acceptance

Acceptance is a major contributor to life satisfaction. Philosophers, religious icons, and other wise sages have shared this view throughout the ages. Most often we think of acceptance in terms of coping with difficult life circumstances that are beyond our control, such as a life-threatening illness, a relationship loss, a natural disaster, a past trauma, a physical limitation, or adverse decisions made by others. Life can take an endless number of twists and turns that can have devastating effects on our quality of life. And in these circumstances, acceptance plays a critical role in coping with adversity. Acceptance, though, doesn't come naturally to most people. Like letting go of control, it must be nurtured and practiced in everyday living.

Michael J. Fox, the Hollywood actor, producer, and writer who was diagnosed with Parkinson's disease at age twenty-nine, is quoted as saying "Acceptance doesn't mean resignation; it means understanding that something is what it is and that there's got to be a way through it." You also may know all too well the hardships and disappointments of life. You may not have a devastating chronic illness, but you have had adversities, maybe even tragedies, that have been crushing. You may have done your best to cope with tragedy and come to realize that you can't change what happened or simply eliminate the pain and suffering by sheer willpower. Possibly you are reminded of this truth by the life experiences you recorded at the beginning of chapter 5. Acceptance, which is the topic of this chapter, is that ability to acknowledge the unpleasantness, the losses and the hurt, that comes into our life, unwanted and uninvited. The healing power of acceptance is best summed up in the first few lines of the Serenity Prayer, attributed to American theologian Reinhold Niebuhr: "God grant me the serenity to accept the things I cannot change; courage to change the things I can; and wisdom to know the difference."

Is there some life difficulty or problem you're facing that needs a strong dose of acceptance?

EXERCISE: Where You Need to Find Acceptance

Take a moment to briefly record the life problem or situation that is having the greatest negative effect on your quality of life.

Your most difficult life circumstance or problem:

_____

_____

_____

Unwanted intrusive thoughts associated with depression and anxiety often stem from difficult or stressful life experiences. If your distressing mental intrusions are linked to a specific problem or situation in your life, your work in this chapter will be helpful.

This chapter focuses on self-acceptance of negative thoughts and feelings, which may be triggered by life stressors over which you have limited control. On the other hand, you may have distressing intrusions that are unassociated with any specific life stressor. Either way, your work on self-acceptance in this chapter will transform your approach to mental and emotional control. You'll also learn how to use mindfulness to deal with personal distress and control over unwanted mental intrusions.

Your ability to use self-acceptance and mindfulness depends on the progress you've made so far in this book. Using self-acceptance and mindfulness will help you do two important things: reduce the personal significance of your intrusions and decrease your mental-control effort and reliance on ineffective control strategies.

Psychologists have increasingly recognized that willingness, acceptance, and mindfulness are beneficial for dealing with a variety of mental health issues as well as promoting life satisfaction and well-being. Fortunately, you're not starting from scratch. The fact that you are reading this workbook shows a strong element of willingness to deal with your emotional problems. The goal in this chapter, then, is to sharpen your focus on self-acceptance and enhance its contribution to your new mental-control approach to distress. To begin looking at how this works, I want to return to Samantha, who was introduced in chapter 3.

Samantha's Story: Learning to Accept

Despite her best intentions, Samantha seemed powerless to overcome her social anxiety. Even the anticipation of a social encounter could cause the most intense feeling of anxiety. These experiences would begin with the intrusive thought *I'll be extremely anxious* and then proceed to other negative thoughts like *I'll embarrass myself* and *People will think there's something wrong with me* and *I'm such a loser for being so fearful.* When that first reminder of anxiety popped into her mind, Samantha tried hard to suppress the thought. She worked at convincing herself that there was nothing to fear, that maybe she wouldn't feel so nervous this time. Sometimes she would ask her mother if she thought she'd be okay if she went to a party. At other times, she tried to calm herself down by meditating and thinking positive thoughts. But none of these strategies were effective. The thoughts of being anxious came roaring back into her mind, and with them came a sense of defeat and despair. Samantha was becoming more and more frustrated by her negative emotions, and she longed for the day when she could be anxiety-free. Samantha couldn't accept herself as a socially anxious person. Instead, she believed a personal transformation was required; she needed to become calm and confident around others. But such a radical change seemed impossible, and so she remained stuck in her anxious state.

What Is Self-Acceptance?

Self-acceptance means being willing to welcome thoughts and feelings we do not want. Such self-acceptance is based on the recognition that everyone experiences negative intrusive thoughts and feelings over which we have less than desired control. Self-acceptance is not unlike accepting negative life stressors or circumstances outside ourself. In both cases, our control is limited, and we are forced to acknowledge that a certain degree of personal pain and suffering is inevitable in this life. Of course, our ability to deal with distressing intrusive thoughts improves if we reduce their personal significance, relinquish excessive mental control, and utilize more effective control strategies. But these interventions can have a positive effect on anxiety or depression only if we're able to exercise a certain level of self-acceptance. As an example, working on self-acceptance played an important role in Samantha's new approach to her social anxiety.

Again, Samantha wanted to feel no anxiety in social situations, but after years of trying to conquer her social fears, she came to the realization that she would always feel some anxiety around others. For Samantha, self-acceptance meant acknowledging her discomfort around others, her heightened self-consciousness, and thoughts of negative evaluation by others. She realized she wasn't going to make a radical change in her personality and suddenly become a self-confident, gregarious extrovert. The challenge for her was to accept in a nonjudgmental manner the continued existence of unwanted anxiety and negative intrusions in social settings. Instead of fighting her social anxiety, she needed to learn a better way to manage her negative thoughts and feelings. So before meeting unfamiliar people, Samantha needed to remind herself to accept her thoughts and feelings, like this:

I know I'm going to feel anxious. Thoughts that I'm making a bad impression and that others are thinking the worst of me will flood my mind. I'll feel awkward, and it will seem like everyone is staring at me. It's okay to think and feel this way. I've learned new ways to deal with the anxiety and intrusive thoughts. I need to work with my negative thoughts and feelings. I need to be myself in these social situations: a person who is shy and somewhat awkward around others.

To get to this place of self-acceptance, Samantha was using tools from a therapeutic intervention called acceptance and commitment therapy (ACT).

Self-Acceptance and ACT

Many psychologists now use ACT as an effective intervention for anxiety and depression (Hayes, Strosahl, and Wilson 2011; Roemer and Orsillo 2009). ACT offers a different approach to our internal experience, that is, to our thoughts and feelings. When distressed, there's a tendency to treat unwanted negative thoughts and emotions as if they were facts, to then try hard to suppress or even avoid the experience, and to become so captivated by our private world that we fail to follow through on actions that contribute to the fulfillment of cherished goals and values. According to ACT, Samantha continues to struggle with social anxiety because she treats the intrusive thought *I'll be so anxious, everyone will think there's something wrong with me* as a fact rather than a thought. Because of this, she tries to suppress the intrusion to quell her anxious feelings, and the anxious intrusion returns, causing Samantha to conclude that her only option is to avoid others. But the avoidance means she fails to make new friends, which is an important personal goal. As a result, Samantha fails to live a full and satisfying life, like making friends and enjoying social activities, because she reacts to her anxious thoughts as a foregone reality rather than as unwanted imaginations in her mind.

ACT offers a solution to this problem of avoidance: change how you relate to unwanted thoughts and feelings. Rather than trying to suppress, control, or avoid negative thoughts and feelings, ACT therapists work on helping you develop a more open, nonjudgmental, and receptive attitude toward your negative inner experience. In other words, you're encouraged to practice self-acceptance: to acknowledge that life is full of pain, suffering, and disappointment which often cannot be eradicated through sheer effort and willpower (Leahy, Tirch, and Napolitano 2011). Because life can be difficult, negative thoughts and feelings are inevitable. The pathway to self-acceptance involves three interrelated parts:

1. Being kinder, more compassionate, and nonjudgmental toward your inner self

2. Learning to be open, receptive, and comfortable with the experience of unwanted thoughts and feelings

3. Viewing negative thoughts and feelings as unpleasant experiences that you can work with rather than fight against

Until now, you may not have considered the importance of self-acceptance. You may have learned to expect a certain amount of pain, suffering, and disappointment in this life, but you've never really thought about it from the perspective of self-acceptance. The next exercise provides an opportunity for you to reflect on your own experience of self-acceptance. This exercise requires that you spend time thinking about your past efforts to deal with a difficult life problem. You'll need a quiet, comfortable location where you can engage in thirty to sixty minutes of reflection without interruption.

EXERCISE: Reflections on Self-Acceptance

Take the following steps to reflect on self-acceptance, and use the worksheet to record your observations:

1. Begin by thinking back to all the ways you've tried to deal with a particular life problem; it can be a problem that you wrote about at the beginning of the chapter. If you don't have a significant life stressor or problem, think about some unwanted thought or feeling you've struggled to accept. In the left-hand column of the worksheet, list various actions you've taken to deal with the life difficulty, unwanted thought, or feeling; for example, if the stressor is being diagnosed with cancer, having obsessive thoughts of doubt, or having recurring bouts of depression, think about all the ways you've tried to deal with the problem.

2. Consider whether you adopted a kind and nonjudgmental attitude toward yourself as you tried to cope with this difficulty. Briefly describe how you showed patience, kindness, and understanding toward yourself in the second column.

3. Then briefly explain in the third column how open you were to unwanted thoughts and feelings as you were dealing with the life difficulty. Did you feel okay with the negative thoughts that popped into your mind while dealing with the stress?

4. In the last column note the extent that you could distance yourself from the negative thoughts associated with the difficulty. Were you able to treat any negative thoughts as simply unpleasant thought occurrences, or did you become distracted by or immersed in your negative thinking?

Self-Acceptance Worksheet

Action Taken to Deal with Unwanted, Difficult Life Situation	Degree of Self-Compassion	Openness to Unwanted Thoughts or Feelings	Ability to Consider Negative Thoughts As Tolerable, Unpleasant Mental Occurrences
1.			
2.			
3.			
4.			
5.			

As you look back on your attempts to deal with your difficult life circumstance, were you able to practice self-acceptance? Could you accept the negative thoughts and feelings that occurred when coping with the life stressor, or did you feel like you were fighting against these unwanted intrusions?

Samantha examined some of the ways she tried to deal with the problem of social anxiety, and she realized self-acceptance was in short supply when trying to cope. She was often impatient with herself and highly self-critical. She tried to stop herself from thinking so negatively, but once the thoughts started, she easily got sidetracked into thinking about how awful she felt when anxious around others.

From your work on this exercise, you too may have concluded that you're not very accepting of the negative experiences in your life. You've been more self-critical than patient and self-compassionate in your attempts to deal with the experiences that make you feel anxious or depressed. You may also have noticed that you're not very open and accepting of the negative intrusive thoughts, images, or memories that pop into your mind. If this is your conclusion, then you'll want to work on promoting self-acceptance.

Promoting Self-Acceptance

When you have a healthy attitude of self-acceptance toward your unwanted negative thoughts and feelings, you'll find it easier to use the mental-control strategies presented in chapter 7. Here are some self-help activities that can boost self-acceptance.

Let Your Mind Wander

People who are self-accepting are also comfortable with the spontaneous, creative part of the mind. On the other hand, if you have very low self-acceptance, you may have difficulty tolerating any thoughts that are unexpected and uncontrollable; you can become so concerned about mental control that even letting your mind wander becomes an anxious experience. Mind wandering is a normal thought process that everyone experiences daily, but people with low self-acceptance can feel uncomfortable when not in control. Thus, ordinary daydreaming, that is, letting your mind wander, becomes an experience that you may avoid if possible.

Better self-acceptance begins with being receptive to letting your mind wander—having an openness and tolerance for any thought that might pop into your head. The next exercise is intended to help you develop a more accepting attitude toward your creative mind, to relinquish directed mental control, and to open your mind to whatever thoughts, images, or memories it may choose to produce. Mind wandering, daydreaming, and other forms of spontaneous thought are usually involuntary, often happening when we least expect it, so to promote greater acceptance of spontaneous thought, it's necessary to become intentional about mind wandering. This exercise of intentional mind wandering will help you build up tolerance of your free-floating, spontaneous mind.

EXERCISE: Intentional Mind Wandering

Over the next week, take a five-minute pause several times a day to let your mind wander. This mind-wandering pause can be done anywhere. It's like taking a few minutes to relax or meditate, except in this case you're taking the time to daydream or let your mind wander on any topic. Begin each pause with a few relaxing breaths. Then simply let your mind wander. Allow yourself to think about whatever pops into your mind. Don't try to control what you think. That is, don't make yourself have certain thoughts and don't try to prevent other thoughts from entering your mind. Just let yourself daydream for the next five minutes or so. At the end of this mind-wandering pause, take a minute to very briefly note your experience on the mind-wandering record. Next rate your overall daily tolerance of the mind-wandering experiences on a 0 to 10 scale, where 0 means no tolerance with spontaneous thoughts to 10 means completely tolerant of the spontaneous thoughts, images, or memories.

Mind-Wandering Record

Date	Mind-Wandering Themes	Level of Tolerance/ Comfort (0 to 10 scale)
Sunday		
Monday		
Tuesday		
Wednesday		
Thursday		
Friday		
Saturday		

After spending a week engaged in intentional mind wandering, how would you evaluate your efforts? As the week progressed, were you more comfortable with letting your mind wander? Did your level of self-acceptance of a wandering mind improve with practice? To gain more insight and understanding from this exercise, take some time to answer these questions in the space provided.

1. Did you have any negative or threatening thoughts pop into your mind during your mind-wandering pauses? If so, jot down the most negative thoughts:

   _____

   _____

   _____

2. If you had negative thoughts, how well did you accept or tolerate them?

   _____

   _____

   _____

3. If you had negative thoughts, was there anything about them that made them intolerable or difficult to accept?

   _____

   _____

   _____

4. Did you have any positive or pleasant intrusions that were associated with high tolerance and comfort? If so, briefly describe them here:

   _____

   _____

   _____

If you want to spend more time with this exercise, you can visit http://www.newharbinger .com/38426 to download other copies of this mind-wandering record.

People differ in their level of comfort with a wandering mind. Samantha, for example, would have no difficulty with this exercise because her unwanted intrusions were very specific to social situations. If you are comfortable with this exercise, then you should proceed to the next exercise on focused mindful acceptance. Alternatively, you may still be uncomfortable with mind wandering because you fear what might happen if you were to let go of mental control. If this is how you feel, you should continue to work with this mind-wandering exercise until you feel more comfortable with an open mind.

It would be good to continue taking note of any unacceptable or distressing thoughts you experience during intentional mind wandering, as you'll want to work on these intrusions in chapter 7. If you've increased your tolerance for a wandering mind, you're making progress toward increasing self-acceptance.

Practice Mindful Acceptance

One of the best ways to strengthen self-acceptance is to practice *mindfulness*, which involves acknowledging the momentary presence of your unwanted thoughts and feelings in a nonjudgmental, receptive manner. Focused mindful acceptance requires a shift in your reaction when feeling distressed. Instead of trying to control your thoughts and feelings, you passively observe how you are thinking and feeling at that moment without any attempt to change your inner experience. For example, Samantha could practice mindful acceptance of the intrusive thought *I'll be so anxious when I meet these people* by saying to herself:

Oh, there's that anxious thought again. Hello, anxious thought. How are you today? I didn't invite you into my mind, but I see you've come anyway. Feel free to stick around if you want. I have a lot of other things to do, so I can't stop and spend a lot of time with you. Instead, my attention must be focused on other activities, but you can stay in the back of my mind. If you demand my attention, I'll only be able to acknowledge that you're still in my mind, but then I'll have to get back to the important tasks of the moment. I don't mean to be rude, but you are an uninvited guest in my mind, so you'll have to put up with my passive and divided attention.

Mindfulness is a popular psychological treatment for a variety of mental health problems. If you've been trained in mindfulness, you can use these skills to increase your self-acceptance of negative intrusive thoughts. If you're unfamiliar with the mindfulness approach, you'll find recommended readings on the topic in the resources section. Whether you're a practitioner of mindfulness or a novice, however, the next exercise can be useful for building up self-acceptance. Mindful acceptance is a strategy you'll want to practice regularly in response to distressing intrusive thoughts and feelings. You can visit http://www.newharbinger.com/38426 to download other copies of the mindful-acceptance record used here.

EXERCISE: Mindful Acceptance

Practice mindful acceptance every day for a couple of weeks, taking these steps repeatedly throughout each day:

1. When aware of feeling distress or being upset, stop what you are doing and focus your attention on your inner experience. Ask yourself, *What am I thinking and feeling at this moment?*

2. Next, imagine you are standing with your arms held open, and you're embracing these difficult, unwanted thoughts, feelings, and sensations. You willingly focus on them without trying to change or alter in any way your inner experience at that moment in time (Teasdale et al. 2014). You allow yourself to fully experience the distressing thoughts and feelings without judgment, without self-criticism, but with ever-present kindness and compassion toward yourself.

3. Hold your attitude of mindful observation for five to ten minutes, and then resume your daily activity.

At the end of each day, use the mindfulness-acceptance record to rate your experience with this strategy, based on your daily experience of practicing mindful acceptance. First rate how often you practiced mindfulness throughout the day; use a scale of 0 to 10, where 0 means not at all (did not practice mindfulness today) and 10 means you always practiced mindful acceptance when you experienced distress. Then rate the overall quality of your self-acceptance, or your ability to tolerate distressing thoughts and feelings; use a scale of 0 to 10, where 0 means you experienced no self-acceptance (could not tolerate the negative experience), and 10 means you experienced complete self-acceptance (were able to embrace the negative thoughts and feelings).

Mindful-Acceptance Record

Day of Week	Rating of Mindful Practice (0 to10)	Rating of Self-Acceptance (0 to 10)
Sunday		
Monday		
Tuesday		
Wednesday		
Thursday		
Friday		
Saturday		

After spending a couple of weeks on mindful acceptance, review the records you've completed. How often did you practice mindful acceptance when feeling distressed? With practice, did you notice whether you were more accepting or more tolerant of your unwanted thoughts and feelings?

If you're practicing mindful acceptance, you should notice a change in how you are dealing with your negative emotional experiences. Your efforts to inhibit negative thoughts, images, or memories should diminish, and you should be taking a more passive, open, and understanding approach to the unwanted thoughts and feelings that intrude into your mind. In other words, you should feel a rise in your general level of patience, tolerance, and compassion toward yourself, as you realize that you are a person who experiences the full scope of life, both the pleasant and the unpleasant.

Wrap-Up

No doubt you're tired from warring against disturbing intrusive thoughts and feelings. You've struggled hard to gain control over your distress, but the harder you try, the worse you feel. Maybe you've gotten to the point where you're fed up with your apparent weakness and inability to pull yourself together. You're ready for something new, a fresh approach to your inner turmoil. But before you can use the new strategies of mental control, it's important to step back from the distress and approach your troubled mind with a greater degree of compassion and acceptance. Nothing good can be achieved by self-punishment and reproach. Rather, tolerance and self-acceptance are the prerequisites for adopting a new perspective on your anxiety or depression. Some of the key points in this chapter are

- Self-acceptance is the willingness to tolerate, even welcome, unwanted intrusive thoughts and feelings.

- Mindful self-acceptance is characterized by an open, nonjudgmental approach to all inner experience.

- Healthy mindful self-acceptance begins with an ability to experience a wandering mind without fear or hesitation.

- Mindful self-acceptance is strengthened by intentionally and repeatedly embracing unwanted thoughts and feelings, allowing yourself to fully experience them without judgment or self-criticism, but with self-compassion.

Chapter 7 will introduce specific mental-control skills that you'll find helpful in dealing with anxiety, depression, obsessions, and other negative emotional states. However, it's important to continue cultivating an attitude of self-acceptance. Detoxification, letting go of excessive and ineffective mental control, and now self-compassion along with tolerance of negative intrusive thoughts and feelings are important pillars of the new science of mental control. You may need to return to previous chapters to refresh your understanding of these important topics as you move on in this workbook. Keeping that in mind, it's time to learn four mental-control strategies that can transform your approach to negative emotion.

CHAPTER 7

Control Skills:
Strategies That Work

Most of us find change difficult. Even when our efforts don't produce the outcome we desire, it's not easy to switch strategies. Our continued reliance on an ineffective coping strategy, for example, is often driven by the desire to avoid short-term pain even at the expense of long-term gain. Say you have a problem with a coworker who's creating tension in the office. As the manager, it's your job to deal with the problem. But confrontation makes you anxious, so you say nothing. The problem continues to fester, creating more stress in your daily work life. The more effective strategy would be to meet with the coworker and deal with the problem head-on. But that too is stressful, and so you continue to manage conflict the old way, with procrastination and avoidance.

Just like when we face problems in the external world, we each have our habitual ways of dealing with the inner world of the mind. Chapter 5 introduced you to several common mental-control strategies that are relatively ineffective for dealing with intrusive thoughts of anxiety and depression. Yet they may be your go-to responses, because they sometimes produce short-term relief even if the end result is long-term distress. Now it's time to reverse the equation: to adopt control strategies that produce genuine improvement in your emotional well-being.

This is a chapter about change and how you can respond more effectively to your unwanted mental intrusions. It focuses on four mental-control strategies that have demonstrated effectiveness for dealing with unwanted thoughts and feelings. First, to ensure that you're ready to work on these new control skills, you'll briefly evaluate the progress you've made already through this workbook. Then you'll learn how to use the new mental-control strategies in your daily experience of personal distress. But before getting started, I want to return to Daniel from chapter 1. Daniel learned to deal more effectively with his obsessions by undertaking radical change in his mental-control strategies.

Daniel's Story: Deflating Excessive Doubt

If you recall from chapter 1, Daniel was often hounded by intrusive doubts over whether he had made a mistake or had been careless in his actions and decision making. When Daniel doubted whether he had locked the door, sent the correct email, been truthful in his conversation, or shut down his computer, his main response was to check over and over or try to reassure himself that everything was all right. But these control strategies were ineffective; soon the doubt returned, and with it came intense feelings of discomfort and uncertainty. So Daniel needed a different approach to his obsessive doubt.

First Daniel learned that his anxiety was caused by a thought and not a real-life situation. He was uncomfortable not because he was actually making mistakes but rather because he was having an intrusive thought of doubt. Second, he worked on reducing his compulsive checking, because checking was only making the obsessive doubt worse. And third, he adopted imaginal exposure as an alternative to compulsive checking. Daniel scheduled a thirty- to forty-five-minute session of daily exposure in which he intentionally recalled thoughts and memories of doubt.

In a typical exposure session, Daniel would think about whether he'd left the house and hadn't locked the door. He imagined driving to work with doubts about whether he'd locked the door flooding his mind. He then thought about an unlocked front door and what would happen if an intruder tried the door. As he visualized this scenario, he thought more broadly about the doubts. If someone really wanted to break into his house, would a locked door stop them? And what would be the worst thing that could happen if an intruder did break in? How would he handle being robbed?

Later in the chapter, you'll learn about imaginal exposure and how to use this strategy to deal with your own distressing mental intrusions. Imaginal exposure is a highly effective strategy for obsessive thinking, but it can be useful for other types of mental intrusions as well. Before we delve into any new mental-control skills, though, you'll want to spend time in the next section reviewing your progress with the workbook.

A Gentle Reminder

By now you've invested considerable time and effort into changing how you understand and cope with the intrusive thoughts, images, and memories that contribute to your anxiety or depression. It's my hope that you've felt some relief from your personal distress by applying the following three pillars of the new science of mental control:

- Detoxifying the emotional significance of unwanted mental intrusions.

- Letting go of excessive mental-control efforts.

- Boosting self-acceptance and tolerance for negative thoughts and feelings.

I encourage you to take a few minutes to complete the next exercise to review your progress. It's a great way to look at the skills you've acquired from the previous chapters and to identify areas of mental control that may require further work.

EXERCISE: Checklist of Progress

Place a checkmark (√) beside the skills you've achieved or leave blank if you believe further work is needed. You can work more on these skills by reviewing the chapters noted in parentheses.

_____   *I'm able to identify the key intrusive thought, image, or memory associated with my experiences of depression, anxiety, obsessions, guilt, or frustration. (See chapters 1 and 3.)*

_____   *I realize my efforts to refrain from (suppress) unwanted intrusive thoughts are counterproductive. (See chapter 2.)*

_____   *I am no longer afraid of losing control of my mind. (See chapter 2.)*

_____   *I understand how I attach unrealistic importance to my unwanted mental intrusions; that is, how I interpret the intrusion as a toxic mental experience. (See chapters 3 and 4.)*

_____   *I have created my own mental-control profile. (See chapter 3.)*

_____   *I now consider the distressing intrusion less personally significant; that is, I'm able to detoxify the intrusion. (See chapter 4.)*

_____   *I can catch myself when I overthink and correct this way of thinking (See chapter 5.)*

_____   *I'm able to let go of excessive mental-control effort. (See chapter 5.)*

_____   *I'm aware of my reliance on maladaptive control strategies. (See chapter 5.)*

_____   *I've developed a more accepting, tolerant attitude toward unwanted distressing thoughts and feelings. (See chapter 6.)*

_____   *I've found mindful self-acceptance helpful. (See chapter 6.)*

These statements represent the main learning objectives of the first six chapters. They are the skills you'll need to adopt the new mental-control strategies presented in this chapter.

I hope that you are feeling encouraged. No matter how many statements you checked off, it's a reminder that you've made at least some positive changes in how you approach intrusive thoughts and feelings. If you've left several statements blank, let this be a gentle reminder that you may need to do more work in these areas. You can either go back now to the relevant chapters to redo some of the exercises or proceed with the current chapter. If you choose to do the latter and then have difficulty practicing the new mental-control skills, consider whether you should spend more time working on the earlier skills.

Daniel realized he still had a strong fear of losing control and had difficulty letting go of excessive control over his doubting intrusions. These issues interfered with his ability to stop his compulsive checking and to practice imaginal exposure. So Daniel decided to do more work on correcting two maladaptive beliefs: that he could lose complete control and that more mental-control effort is better than less mental-control effort.

Four Effective Control Strategies

Now that you've completed the skills self-audit, it's time to consider four effective mental-control strategies. You can expect some strategies to be more helpful to you than others. I encourage you to do the exercises to learn how to use each strategy, so you'll have some personal experience before choosing the strategies that work best for you.

Focused Distraction

The most effective control strategy for a wide range of distressing thoughts and feelings is *focused distraction*, an intentional mental-control strategy in which we shift our attention to a single highly engaging idea, memory, or activity that diverts attention away from the unwanted intrusive thought (Wegner 1994b). Imagine you are waiting for the results of a medical test, and you keep having the intrusive thought, *What if the test is positive and I have cancer?* In response, you try to distract yourself, but your mind keeps wandering from one topic to the next. This would be unfocused distraction (see chapter 5 for further discussion). A more effective strategy is to focus your attention on a single idea or task that brings you pleasure, such as thinking about spring gardening and what you would like to plant. Naturally, thoughts of the medical test will continue to recur, but each time you gently bring your attention back to the garden. Using focused distraction, you avoid creating multiple cues for the intrusion. Research on mental control indicates that the negative effects of suppression diminish significantly when people use focused distraction (Najmi, Riemann, and Wegner 2009).

If you've been using unfocused distraction as an automatic response to distressing thoughts, then it will help to shift your distraction strategy to the focused approach. Doing this will take some mental effort and practice.

DISTRACTOR LIST

The first step is to generate a list of potential distractors, because you can't leave distraction to chance, that is, wait until you have an intrusion and then pick the first thought that pops into your mind as the distractor. If you did wait, then you'd be more likely to select an ineffective distractor, especially if you're in a negative mood state. You'd then be forced to try another distractor, and before long, you'd be back in unfocused distraction. To prevent this from happening, you need to have a list of effective distractors to call on when having distressing intrusive thoughts and feelings. The next exercise provides some guidance.

EXERCISE: The Distractor List

Use the worksheet to construct your list of potential distractors. In the memories column, record five to ten memories or past experiences that involve success, happiness, or something you value or cherish. Next, list several pleasurable or positive activities, hobbies, or leisure pursuits, such as traveling, in the activities column. Finally, write down some positive daydreams, hopes, and aspirations in the third column. You'll want to choose distractors that are engaging and that you find absorbing when they enter your mind. When adding a distractor to your list, consider the following:

Does this thought, memory, or activity have high personal value? Thoughts, memories, or activities that represent something important to us are better at holding our attention.

Is this a moderately challenging activity? Mental or physical activities that are moderately challenging are better at grabbing our attention.

Is the thought, memory, or activity associated with success, positive expectation, and a strong sense of personal control? If the answer is yes, it will be more likely to capture your attention.

Make sure you have several distractors in each category. If you have trouble thinking of distractors, consider consulting with your partner, therapist, or someone who knows you well.

Your Distractor List

Memories	Activities	Daydreams, Aspirations
1.		
2.		
3.		
4.		
5.		
6.		
7.		
8.		
9.		
10.		

If you're like most people, you've probably never evaluated your thoughts in terms of their distractibility. When you do try to use distraction, it's on the spur of the moment, so sitting down and planning your distraction strategy may seem unnatural. But it's important to do if you're serious about correcting your tendency to choose less effective distractors.

When Daniel did this exercise, he knew he needed a list of excellent distractors to call on when he had an intrusive thought of doubt, so he could resist his checking compulsion. For memories, Daniel listed college graduation, his wedding day, his first child's birth, moving into his current house, a recent news story that concerned him, and promotion to be a high-level manager at work. His list of positive and pleasurable activities included a furniture-refinishing project, golfing, a recent Caribbean cruise, barbecuing steaks on a sunny summer day, and taking a leisurely drive. His most engaging daydreams and aspirations were thinking about retirement, renovating his house, buying a new car, visiting his son in Europe, spending a weekend skiing with some friends, and planning a surprise birthday party for his best friend.

TAKING ACTION WITH DISTRACTION

Once you've created your distractor list, it's time to put your plan into action. Figure 7.1 illustrates how to use focused distraction to manage your mental intrusions.

The focused distraction steps presented in figure 7.1 are not natural responses to unwanted mental intrusions but very intentional responses. That is, instead of reacting to a distressing intrusion the way you usually do, you choose to do this instead. You first mindfully accept the intrusion and then remind yourself why this intrusion is insignificant (nontoxic). Using focused distraction, you then think deeply on a distractor that you've chosen from your distractor list. You then focus on breathing and calm, and then move on to engage in a distracting activity.

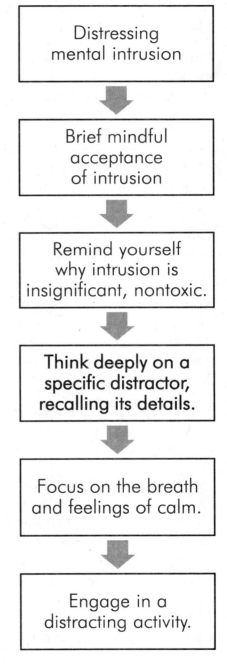

Figure 7.1.
The Focused-Distraction Strategy

123

You'll notice that the success of focused distraction depends on several other effective control strategies besides generating a good distractor. Acceptance of the intrusion, being reminded of its insignificance, briefly focusing on your breath or some other calming response, and finally engaging in a distracting activity are all elements in effective focused distraction. There are several features of this strategy to keep in mind.

Practice, practice, practice. Focused distraction may look simple, but it's harder than you think. Don't get discouraged if at first it doesn't seem to work. Keep practicing with a variety of distractors. Remember, the more frequent and intense the mental intrusion, the more practice you'll need.

Engage in acceptance and reinterpretation. Focused distraction can succeed only if you've already learned to tolerate the unwanted intrusion and have reappraised the thought, image, or memory as less personally significant (that is, nontoxic).

Focus your reflection. As you turn your attention to the distractor, you will need to bring to your mind detailed information, so you can fully concentrate on the distractor. For distraction to work, you must be able to retrieve enough information to become absorbed in your mental distractor.

Keep it brief. Focused distraction is a brief intervention. You'll probably find you can focus on the distractor for only five to ten minutes. As you are thinking, you can switch your focus from the distractor to your breath, taking slow, deep diaphragmatic breaths. Alternating your attention between your breathing and the distractor will improve your ability to concentrate on the distractor.

Expect intrusive interruptions. No doubt you'll find that the unwanted intrusion returns. This is to be expected. Simply welcome the intrusion, sit with it for a couple of seconds, and then gently bring your attention back to the distractor.

Get up and do something. It is important to end the focused distraction with an activity. Sitting for prolonged periods and doing mental-control exercises is not a good idea. Instead, it is important to reengage in your daily activities.

Again, you'll need to work at shifting from unfocused to focused distraction. To encourage your efforts, you may want to keep a daily diary. The next exercise is a useful way to keep track of your focused distraction experiences.

EXERCISE: Your Focused-Distraction Diary

Take a few minutes each evening to reflect on your daily experience with focused distraction. Write down the date on the worksheet, rate your experience that day with focused distraction, including the frequency of focused distraction (how often you attempted it), the distractibility level of the distractors, overall success in reducing frequency and duration of the intrusion, and overall success in reducing negative mood. Use a scale of 0 to 4, where 0 is none, 1 is minimal, 2 is somewhat, 3 is moderate, and 4 is very much.

Date	Frequency of Focused Distraction (0 to 4)	Distractibility Level of the Distractors (0 to 4)	Success in Reducing Frequency and Duration of Intrusion (0 to 4)	Success in Reducing Negative Mood (0 to 4)

After the first week of practicing focused distraction, take some time to review what you've written on your focused-distraction worksheet. If you rated yourself in the 0 to 2 range in the frequency column, then you're not practicing focused distraction enough to master this mental-control strategy. This is especially true if you had frequent unwanted intrusions during the week. It means you are missing opportunities to practice focused distraction.

The remaining three ratings in the focused-distraction worksheet capture various aspects of the effectiveness of your intervention. The second column is your assessment of the distractibility quality of your distractors. Were you using the most potent distractors in response to your unwanted intrusions? The third and fourth columns refer to the success of the distraction. Did you have fewer problems with unwanted intrusions and did you experience a reduction in personal distress when you were using focused distraction? If your ratings were consistently low in these last columns, it may be due to insufficient practice, or you may be relying on relatively weak distractors with low distractibility potential. If you want to continue tracking your progress with focused distraction, you can download other copies of this focused-distraction diary by visiting http://www.newharbinger.com/38426.

If you're not pleased with your distraction efforts, you may want to try fixing the problem before concluding it doesn't work for you. For example, you may need to identify more potent distractors that will capture your attention more completely. Also, distraction is more likely to be effective after you've reduced the significance of the intrusion, adopted an attitude of acceptance, and developed a laissez-faire take-it-or-leave-it approach to its control.

Thought Postponement and Imaginal Exposure

The next two mental-control strategies are interrelated; you use them together to effectively confront unwanted intrusive thoughts and feelings. Using these two strategies is like being confronted with a difficult situation and telling yourself, *Bring it on! Throw your worst at me. I can take it!* You're taking that same attitude toward your distressing intrusive thoughts and feelings, and it's as if you were talking back, *Okay, intrusion. I can't stop you from popping into my mind. I realize that the harder I try to suppress you, the fiercer you become. I've come to understand that you are far less significant and threatening than I first thought. I accept that I'm stuck with you. So, bring it on. Let's have it out right here and now.*

With thought postponement, the first of these two strategies, you tell yourself not to respond to the intrusion when it pops into your mind but to save your response for a later scheduled time when you will intentionally focus on the intrusion. The second strategy, imaginal exposure, is the planned session when you intentionally generate the intrusion. You first encountered imaginal exposure in chapter 4 where it was introduced as a strategy to reinforce belief in your nontoxic reinterpretation of an intrusive thought. In this chapter, you will use imaginal exposure to reduce negative emotion associated with the thought. You may want to review the section on exposure-based detoxification to refresh your memory of the procedure.

Thought postponement and imaginal exposure were first proposed by Dr. Thomas Borkovec at Pennsylvania State University and are now two of the most effective components of CBT for worry (Clark and A. T. Beck 2012; Roemer and Borkovec 1993). Imaginal exposure is an excellent mental-control strategy for intrusive thoughts that are repetitive and highly anxiety-provoking. It's well suited for intrusions associated with obsessive thinking and worry. However, it's not appropriate for the mental intrusions that feature in depression or guilt. Here's a scenario to show you how thought postponement and imaginal exposure can work together.

THOUGHT POSTPONEMENT EXAMPLE

Imagine you go to work one morning, and the entire office is abuzz with rumors that the company is under threat of a hostile takeover. You know this means a fresh round of layoffs, and as a fifty-five-year-old middle manager, you are extremely vulnerable. Over the next few days as the uncertainty mounts, you are plagued by unwanted intrusive thoughts of losing your job. The intrusion is simple but gut-wrenching. The thought *I'm going to lose my job* hits you hard, triggering a fresh round of worries about finances and unemployment, as you imagine the shame and guilt you'll feel when telling friends and family of your calamity. To achieve control over the intrusion, you practice thought postponement and imaginal exposure.

Whenever you have the intrusive thought of losing your job, you immediately acknowledge the mental intrusion. You remind yourself that it's okay to have such thoughts; that it's perfectly understandable given the circumstances. You then tell yourself that tonight you'll spend time thinking more deeply about losing your job. If there is something different about your current experience of the intrusion, you'll write it down, so you'll remember to think about this in your imaginal-exposure session. You detoxify the intrusion in the following way: *Everyone in the office, including me, is worried about layoffs. Having this intrusion doesn't mean I'm more likely to get laid off. Instead I can use this intrusive thought productively and take some positive steps to prepare for an uncertain future. Millions of people have been laid off and have survived it. So can I.* You then tell yourself to get back to your work or whatever tasks you were doing. If the intrusion returns again and again, you restate your intention to think on it later.

IMAGINAL-EXPOSURE EXAMPLE

Because unwanted intrusions of job loss have been foremost in your mind, you plan to spend thirty minutes each evening between 8:00 and 8:30 intentionally thinking about losing your job. You find a quiet place where you won't be distracted or interrupted. You begin the imaginal-exposure session with two to three minutes of controlled diaphragmatic breathing to feel somewhat relaxed and focused on the task at hand. You then bring to mind thoughts about losing your job. You review any notes you might have taken during thought postponement to make sure you're generating different variations of the intrusive job-loss theme. You might use visual imagery to imagine getting your pink slip. You might imagine telling your wife and children that you've lost your job, and think of the various consequences of losing your job, like job hunting, living off your savings, being at home alone, and so on. As you think deeply about why you might be the one to lose your job, you try to feel the anxiety, discouragement, and sadness that you'd experience if this happened. If you get distracted from the job-loss theme—if unrelated thoughts flit through your mind—you gently bring your attention back to the distressing thought. You continue thinking deeply about your potential job loss. At the end of thirty minutes, you remind yourself that it's time to stop and that tomorrow evening you can pick up where you left off. You end the session with an extra five minutes of relaxed, controlled breathing. After this, you engage in some meaningful activity that brings you back to the present moment.

These two examples illustrate the basic steps that you should use any time a distressing thought intrudes. Always practice thought postponement and imaginal exposure together: when you have a distressing intrusive thought, you immediately respond with thought postponement. You can use the thought-postponement checklist in the next exercise to ensure that you are using this mental-control procedure effectively. For further practice, you can also visit http://www.newharbinger.com/38426 to download other copies of this thought-postponement checklist.

EXERCISE: Thought-Postponement Checklist

Two or three times a week, go through the checklist to determine whether you've been using thought postponement correctly. Place a checkmark (√) beside the steps that you are doing regularly. Leave blank any that require more work, so you can improve your thought post-ponement skills.

_____   Acknowledge the intrusion.

_____   Practice self-acceptance instead of self-criticalness for having the intrusion (see chapter 6).

_____   Use the mental-intrusion diary (from chapter 3) to record the intrusion.

_____   Remind yourself that you'll think deeply on the intrusion later.

_____   Focus on the insignificance reinterpretation you developed for the intrusion (see chapter 4).

_____   Return your attention to the task at hand.

_____   If the intrusion returns, repeat the previous steps.

Thought postponement is not an effective mental-control strategy unless it's followed by imaginal exposure. Because of this, you'll want to work on both strategies simultaneously.

But don't be surprised if your first attempts with thought postponement prove difficult. Like Daniel, you may need to do more work on detoxification before you can engage in thought postponement.

For imaginal exposure to be effective, you'll need to schedule daily thirty-minute exposure sessions for at least two weeks. It's best to do this at a regular time each day. You'll need a quiet, comfortable location where you won't be interrupted. You'll also want to keep your mental-intrusion diary handy as a reminder of which thoughts you'll need to recall.

Here are some guidelines for how to conduct your imaginal-exposure sessions.

1. Begin the session with five minutes of relaxed diaphragmatic breathing.

2. Bring the unwanted intrusion to your mind, consulting the entries recorded in your mental-intrusion diary (from chapter 3).

3. Reflect on every detail of the intrusion, including possible consequences.

4. Alternate your attention between your thoughts and the associated feeling.

5. If your attention wanders, gently bring it back to the intrusion.

6. Stop at the end of thirty minutes, and remind yourself that tomorrow you can pick up where you left off.

7. End the session with an extra five minutes of relaxed, controlled breathing.

It will help to record the quality of your exposure sessions in an imaginal-exposure record. Before doing the next exercise, you can visit http://www.newharbinger.com/38426 to download additional copies of the imaginal-exposure record.

EXERCISE: Imaginal-Exposure Record

Complete this form at the end of each imaginal-exposure session. Write down the date, the duration of the session, and the content of the intrusive thought. Then indicate how clearly you recalled the intrusion and the average level of distress experienced during the exposure session. Use a 0 to 10 scale to rate your recall ability, where 0 is you were unable to think about the intrusion and 10 is you could think about the intrusion as clearly as when it spontaneously pops into your mind. Use a 0 to 10 scale to rate your average distress level, where 0 is you experienced no distress during the session and 10 is you were as distressed during the session as you are when the intrusion occurs spontaneously.

Date of Session	Duration of Session (minutes)	Intrusive Thought Content During Imaginal Exposure	Quality of Intrusion Recall (0 to 10)	Average Level of Distress (0 to 10)

After two weeks of thought postponement and imaginal exposure, review your entries in the imaginal-exposure record. Were you able to postpone your response to the intrusion when it occurred spontaneously? Did your level of distress decline the more you engaged in intentional imaginal exposure? Most people find that the significance and distress associated with an unwanted intrusive thought, image, or memory changes dramatically when they take control and intentionally generate the thought.

Thought postponement and imaginal exposure were Daniel's primary mental-control strategies for his obsessions. He'd tell himself to hold off on the doubt for now, and then in the evening he'd review all the times he'd doubted throughout the day. Using thought postponement, he actually discovered that the urgency and distress that he first experienced with the intrusion tended to disappear by the time he got to his imaginal doubting session. He could think much more clearly about the doubt during the exposure session, and he discovered new ways to organize his daily activities to minimize the occurrence of doubt.

Do you find that using postponement and intentional exposure is helping you to cope better with your anxiety or obsessions? Imaginal exposure is a great way to take control of distressing intrusive thoughts and feelings that involve concerns about future threat and uncertainty. As a reminder, imaginal exposure can make depression and guilt worse, so don't use it with those types of intrusions.

Self-Affirmation

The final mental-control strategy, *self-affirmation*, involves recognizing your positive qualities and attributes, so you view yourself as adaptively and morally competent, good, and capable (Steele 1988; Wegner 2011). Describing yourself in positive terms or receiving positive feedback about your value tends to improve your mental control over unwanted thoughts (Koole and van Knippenberg 2007). Self-affirmation is expected to be especially helpful for negative intrusions associated with guilt and depression but only when it's preceded by detoxification of the intrusion. That is, thinking about yourself in positive terms will only be therapeutic after you've been able to reinterpret the significance and validity of the original negative intrusion. So how might you tap into self-affirmation to control your negative intrusive thoughts?

Essentially there are two steps to the self-affirmation process in mental control. The first step is to generate a list of positive characteristics and attributes that you can recall when having unwanted intrusive thoughts. The second step is to practice replacing the intrusive thought with a self-affirmation reminder during periods of distress.

EXERCISE: Positive-Attributes Worksheet

To build a self-affirmation list, start by considering important areas of your life. Write down two to three of your positive attributes within each of these domains, as they are listed on the worksheet: work, family or intimate relationships, friendships and social sphere, health and physical fitness, leisure, recreation, and fun, community and citizenship, and spirituality or religious faith. For example, when you think of family, you might describe your positive attributes as being loving, trustworthy, loyal, and understanding. Next, rate each attribute for how much you believe it applies to you. Use a 1 to 10 scale, where 1 is you believe you have this attribute only minimally, to 10 is you believe you are very strong in this attribute. Finally, provide some specific examples of how you express this attribute. If you tend to be quite negative and self-critical, you can ask your partner, a friend, or even your therapist to help you with this exercise.

List of Positive Attributes	Rating Attribute (0 to 10)	Specific Examples of Attribute
Work:		
Family/Intimate Relationships:		
Friendships/Social Sphere:		
Health/Physical Fitness:		
Leisure/Recreation/Fun:		

Community/Citizenship:		
Spirituality/Religious Faith:		

Once you've completed the positive-attributes worksheet, review the attributes you listed in the worksheet and circle the ones that you rated as strongly relevant. These are the attributes you'll want to use as replacement thoughts when you experience distressing intrusive thoughts.

Now you are ready to begin using self-affirmation to counter distressing thoughts. When you feel upset by an intrusive thought, you focus on one of your highlighted attributes and take a few minutes to reflect on personal experiences that reflect this attribute. Say honesty is one of your attributes, and you have depressive intrusive thoughts like *I'm failing at everything.* When this thought pops into your mind, you remember that you're an honest person. But when you think of honesty, you'll need to recall the many ways you've been an honest person; that is, to feel affirmed, you will need to elaborate on your positive attribute (see examples in the positive-attributes worksheet). This is the only way that self-affirmation can counter the distressing intrusion.

Daniel, for example, listed reliability in his job as one of his positive attributes. So, when he had a doubting intrusion, he brought to mind the many ways he's been a reliable employee for more than twenty years. He recalled occasions when he responded to the request of coworkers for assistance. Having concrete examples of reliability meant that Daniel could think deeply about this positive attribute. This insured that his self-affirmation became an effective distractor from his distressing intrusive thought.

Self-affirmation along with the other strategies introduced in this chapter can help you manage your unwanted intrusive thoughts. But these strategies are most effective when combined with the control skills discussed in chapters 3 through 6: self-discovery, mental detoxification, letting go, and mindful self-acceptance. At this point, you may want to look back at the mental-control profile you created in chapter 3 and at the work you completed in subsequent chapters. Are you using the right tools to manage your negative emotions, or do you need to go back and work on other skills?

As this chapter closes, you've completed the workbook's presentation of the mental-control approach to personal distress. If you have done all the exercises and worksheets, then you've been engaged in a different approach to anxiety, depression, guilt, frustration, and other negative emotions. If you've been applying these mental-control strategies and yet feel dissatisfied with the results, you may need to do some troubleshooting (see the appendix).

Wrap-Up

This chapter highlighted some of the most effective mental-control strategies for dealing with unwanted thoughts and feelings associated with anxiety, depression, and obsessions:

- Focused distraction, or shifting attention to a single competing thought, memory, or activity, is an effective strategy for breaking the grip of prolonged distressing intrusive thoughts and memories.

- Using thought postponement and imaginal exposure to intentionally confront distressing thoughts and feelings is an excellent approach for reducing the emotional intensity of intrusions related to obsessions, anxiety, and worry.

- The self-affirmation strategy, which involves focusing intently on your positive attributes, can counter the negative effects of unwanted mental intrusions associated with depression, guilt, and other negative emotions.

You've been working on taking a new approach to decreasing your unwanted distressing intrusive thoughts and their associated feelings. However, psychologists increasingly realize that reducing negative thoughts and feelings is not enough to enhance life satisfaction. Building positive thoughts and feelings is also critical for improving your quality of life. Chapter 8 considers how the mental-control approach can be redirected to capitalize on the spontaneous mental intrusions that make possible momentary states of positive affect or happiness.

Maximizing Positive Intrusions

Who wouldn't want to feel more positive and less negative? Positive emotions like joy, affection, contentment, and pride make us feel energized and more engaged in life. Moreover, happy people have better physical and mental health, they are more successful in life, have more satisfying relationships, and are better able to cope with life's challenges (Lyubomirsky, King, and Diener 2005). No wonder pursuit of life satisfaction is such an important human endeavor. And yet, taking hold of happiness can be difficult and elusive for so many people. When positive feelings do arise, they can evaporate quickly, leaving us feeling empty and disappointed. Often our efforts to prolong positive thoughts and feelings end far too quickly. Before we know it, the negativity returns and we must wait for another moment of positive feeling to break through the stresses and burden of daily living.

EXERCISE: What Is Happiness?

What does happiness mean to you? Take a couple of minutes to respond to these questions.

1. What is happiness?

   _____

   _____

2. What would need to happen in your life to have more positive thoughts and feelings?

   _____

   _____

At the end of the chapter, you'll return to these questions to see if your answers have changed.

Decades of social science research have shed new light on the topic of happiness, or what psychologists now call *subjective well-being* or *life satisfaction* (Diener 2000; Diener et al. 1999). Happiness involves a general evaluation of life, the level of satisfaction attained in various life domains like work and family, and the experience of positive and negative mood (Diener 2000). Happy people are very satisfied with their life, they experience frequent and intense positive moods and less negative emotion, they feel mildly positive most of the time, and they feel quite content, even fulfilled, in their work, family, leisure time, and other aspects of their life. As well, they tend to be more optimistic, feel in control, and generally are worry-free (Cummins and Nistico 2002; Lyubomirsky, King, and Diener 2005). And yet, people differ greatly in their tendency to be positive or feel satisfied in life. Genetic and personality differences play an important role in determining whether you're a happy or unhappy person. Like Soon-Yi in the following example, you may be struggling with negativity and unhappiness and wonder if life satisfaction and well-being are truly elusive for you.

Soon-Yi's Story: A Life of Quiet Discontent

Soon-Yi felt frustrated but at the same time perplexed by her chronic unhappiness. No matter what she did or how hard she tried to think positively, she continued to feel a depth of unhappiness that defied explanation. Soon-Yi was the first to admit that she had no excuse for her low mood and dissatisfaction. As a thirty-two-year-old business executive with a large multinational insurance company, she was successful, prosperous, and healthy. She had several close friends and was in a committed relationship. Despite her comfortable life and many successes, happiness eluded Soon-Yi. She read an endless number of self-help books that told her to think positively, be more grateful for the blessings in her life, invest more time in the lives of others, dedicate herself to love and relationships, and the like. But despite this sound advice and Soon-Yi's best efforts, happiness still seemed fleeting at best. Clearly, her approach was not working. A different strategy was needed.

Like Soon-Yi, you may be committed to being more positive, but you're struggling. Discontent and pessimism come more naturally, and no matter what you do, you always seem to return to the negative. If you've experienced difficult life circumstances, had a traumatic loss in your life, or have a diagnosable mental health condition, your unhappy state is understandable. But if this is not the case, you may find the inability to live joyfully hard to understand.

Whatever the cause, you'll find in this chapter another important pathway to achieving less negativity in thought, feeling, and action. For you need to work not only on reducing negativity but also on encouraging the positive. This chapter emphasizes one skill essential to improving life satisfaction, that is, the ability to harness positive intrusive thoughts and feelings. It will give you several steps to increase your focus on the positive. The starting point is discovering the magnitude of your natural tendency to experience happiness, which is called *baseline happiness*. Next, you will learn how to harness your daily experiences of spontaneous positive thought and feeling to improve your general well-being. Finally, you will learn how reflection, memory cueing, and gratitude can enrich the inner world of spontaneous pleasant thought.

Living a more satisfied life, of course, is not just a matter of strategy. We all have a different starting point when it comes to our potential to nurture positive well-being and greater satisfaction in life.

How Positive Are You?

Like most people, you may feel mildly positive much of the time, but your positive mood fluctuates and may be quite transient compared to feelings of negativity (Diener, Lucas, and Scollon 2006; Fredrickson and Losada 2005). Alternatively, you may be struggling to feel even an occasional moment of happiness. Research indicates there are large differences among people in their tendency for positive affect (Diener et al. 1999). It may be that like Soon-Yi, you've concluded you're destined for a life of misery. Your experiences of positive feelings tend to be infrequent and rather tepid, and when life difficulties occur, it takes you longer to bounce back. No doubt you've tried hard to cheer up or "think more positively," but nothing seems to work, and you're practically ready to give up. Regardless of where you find yourself on the positivity scale, there are two important facts to keep in mind.

One is that our feelings change quickly from one moment to the next (Diener, Lucas, and Scollon 2006). Even the happiest person has some negative emotion, and people who are depressed can have occasional moments of positive feeling. This means that we can influence our emotions for better or worse, regardless of whether our natural inclination is to be positive or negative. The other important fact to remember is that we each have a different starting point on the positivity or happiness scale. Because of this difference you need to measure your progress against yourself rather than other people. The critical question to ask yourself is this: *Since committing myself to a greater concern about my emotional health, am I experiencing more or less positive emotion in my life?*

Before you can start using the positive skills in this chapter, you'll need a better sense of your natural inclination for happiness, or a positive outlook: your *positivity baseline*. This is the general level of happiness you experience without any conscious effort to feel better. You can use the following checklist to obtain a rough estimate of your positivity baseline.

EXERCISE: The Positivity Checklist

Below is a series of statements that deal with general life experiences. Read each statement and place a checkmark (√) next to it if it describes you, and leave it blank if it doesn't.

_____   *Generally I feel satisfied with my life.*

_____   *I often experience feelings of joy, contentment, pride, and amusement.*

_____   *I'm generally optimistic about my future.*

_____   *I rarely worry about the future.*

_____   *My negative feelings, like guilt, sadness, anxiety and anger, are infrequent.*

_____   *I experience a high level of meaning and satisfaction from my work.*

_____   *Most of the time I feel in control of my life.*

_____   *I have close and loving relationships.*

_____   *My life is full of meaning and purpose.*

_____   *I consider myself a good person with as much worth and value as others.*

When completing the checklist, did you feel like the items described you well, or did they seem completely opposite to your character? It can be difficult to do this type of self-evaluation, because most of us would like to check all the boxes. However, it's important to be honest with yourself. If you checked six or more statements, it's likely you're a generally happy or positive person.

If you found it difficult to check any statements, you probably tend toward negativity. But don't feel discouraged if your positivity score is low. You can use the skills in this chapter to raise your happiness level. It may take more effort to improve your mood to the middle range of the positivity scale than it would if your baseline was initially higher, but nevertheless, you can increase your positivity.

The important point is that you are making progress on your commitment to improve your emotional life. Soon-Yi, for example, found that only two statements applied to her: she felt that her work was meaningful and that she had control over her life most of the time. Although this gave her a low positivity baseline, the checklist helped Soon-Yi adopt more realistic targets for increasing her happiness level. It also showed her which areas of her life needed improvement.

The remainder of this chapter focuses on two aspects of happiness alluded to in the checklist: boosting the frequency of positive emotion and reducing the frequency of negative feelings. If you were unable to check the statements *I often experience feelings of joy, contentment, pride, and amusement* and *My negative feelings, like guilt, sadness, anxiety and anger, are infrequent*, then you will find the positivity skills discussed below especially relevant.

Catching Your Positive Feelings

A Canadian bank once ran the tagline, "You're richer than you think." What if you had more positive emotion, that is, more moments of happiness, than you realized? Everyone experiences moments of happiness—sudden and unexpected waves of good feeling—although some people experience more than others. You may have noticed that these flashes of positive emotion elicit a momentary spike of happiness. Actually, these bursts of positive emotion play a critical role in personal well-being because they boost self-confidence and energize us to deal with the demands of daily living. Therefore, increasing the frequency and impact of positive intrusive thoughts and feelings is an important pathway to greater happiness and well-being.

Unfortunately, experiences of spontaneous positive emotion tend to be brief, sometimes disappearing the instant we ask, *Why do I feel so good?* If you could process these naturally occurring positive mood shifts more deeply, however, they would have a bigger impact on your level of happiness. To get the most from these positive feelings, the first step is to pay more attention to sudden moments of pleasant emotion. This can be done by journaling the naturally occurring happy moments that intrude into your daily life.

Soon-Yi discovered she was experiencing more positive emotion than she had realized. To improve her awareness of these spontaneous expressions of positive thought and feeling, she kept a happiness journal over a two-week period. Although it took time to hone her journaling skills, Soon-Yi learned to record times when she felt good, the types of thoughts that flooded her mind during those times, and the positive emotions that best described her experience. She discovered that her positive emotion experiences often involved pride, interest, and challenges, that most of her positive emotion was happening at work, and that it usually involved intrusive thoughts of inspiration and achievement. To improve her level of happiness, Soon-Yi needed to work on developing a greater appreciation of her positive moments and to expand her range of positive experiences beyond achievement.

Soon-Yi did two things to improve her awareness of daily happiness. First, she tracked moments of positive feeling by writing them in her happiness journal. Second, she worked on paying closer attention to the intrusive thoughts associated with her pleasant feelings; these *positive mental intrusions* are thoughts, images, and memories with pleasant, amusing, or uplifting themes that cause a heightened sense of well-being. The thought content of positive mental intrusions is practically limitless and tends to be unique to each of us and our life experiences. Unlike negative intrusive thoughts, our unexpected and spontaneous positive intrusions are wanted mental interruptions. Here are some examples:

139

- Awareness of the beauty, goodness, or vitality of the moment

- A memory of past experience of success, love, fun, reward, or accomplishment

- A sudden inspiration, moment of creativity, or resolution to a problem or challenge

- Recognition of being accepted, affirmed, or loved by others

- Appreciation of your own positive personal characteristics

- A sense of gratitude for life

- A hopeful expectancy for the future

Like Soon-Yi, you may be experiencing positive thoughts but you aren't fully aware of their presence in your mind. The next exercise will help.

EXERCISE: Emphasizing the Positive

Think back to the last time you felt happy. Write down two or three recent positive thoughts, fantasies, or memories that suddenly popped into your mind during that experience of happiness.

1. First positive mental intrusion: _____

2. Second positive mental intrusion: _____

3. Third positive mental intrusion: _____

If you were able to come up with positive mental intrusions, great! But don't be too concerned if you were unable to recall a recent positive intrusive thought. We tend to remember the thoughts that are consistent with our mood state, so if you've been feeling down, anxious, or frustrated, it's likely you're paying far more attention to negative thoughts and feelings than to positive ones. You are probably having some positive intrusions, but they are not getting your attention.

The best way to raise your awareness of positive thoughts and feelings is to keep a happiness journal. If you find this hard to do at first, remember that you're working on boosting your level of life satisfaction and contentment, and one of the best ways to get started is to increase your awareness and appreciation of momentary happiness. Keeping a positivity journal can help you achieve better balance in your emotional state.

EXERCISE: Your Positivity Journal

Record your experiences of momentary positive feeling on the worksheet. Write down the date and time, and then in the next two columns, briefly describe the circumstance in which it occurred and the main thought, image, or memory that popped into your mind when feeling happy. In the final column, describe your feelings in terms of joy, peace, contentment, pride, elation, satisfaction, love, excitement, or another word that best describes the pleasant feeling you experienced.

Date and Time	Where I Was, With Whom, Doing What	Positive Intrusive Thought, Image, or Memory	Pleasant Feeling Experienced

After you've made several entries in the positivity journal, take a few minutes to review and evaluate your journaling experience. Was it difficult to break down your positive emotion into the different categories of situations, intrusive thoughts, and feelings? Were you able to identify the positive mental intrusions that were key to your momentary happiness? As your skill at journaling improves with practice, your awareness of momentary pleasant emotion will increase.

Learning to pay more attention to positive intrusions is so important to creating happiness and well-being that I recommend you continue with this journaling exercise throughout the remainder of this chapter. In fact, the positivity skills discussed next are based on having greater awareness of positive intrusive thoughts and feelings. You can visit http://www.newhar binger.com/38426 to download more copies of this positivity journal.

Active Reflection

Being aware of your positive thoughts and feelings is a good beginning. To have a lasting impact on your sense of life satisfaction, however, it is also important to fully appreciate the positive moment and to process pleasant thoughts and feelings as deeply as possible, to maximize their emotional impact. Think of it as squeezing as much as you can out of your moments of positivity. Few of us do this naturally. Instead we get caught up in the cares of our day or pay more attention to all the negativity that floods our mind. It takes real effort and determination to increase your awareness and appreciation of positivity. This can be accomplished by learning the skill of *active reflection*, which has three components, or steps, summarized by the acronym STP: stop, think, and ponder.

Soon-Yi found active reflection of her positive intrusive thoughts and feelings to be difficult at first. Reflecting on the negative came more naturally to her, and it seemed strange and somewhat phony to practice the three steps of active reflection. But with practice, Soon–Yi experienced its benefits.

This first step—*Stop*—is based on your work in the positivity journal. Stop refers to the act of identifying positive intrusive thoughts and feelings the instant you are conscious of them. The second step—*Think*—involves the use of mindfulness-based strategies to pay full attention to the positive intrusive thought, image, or memory. The third step—*Ponder*—consists of various cognitive strategies to more fully understand the positive intrusion and its implication for the self. The next exercise offers a method you can use regularly to develop your active-reflection skills. You can actively reflect in response to a sudden feeling of positive emotion or do it later when reviewing your positivity journal. Note that it's important to keep your active-reflection sessions brief, so this skill becomes an automatic response to spontaneous positive emotion. After five minutes or so of active reflection, return to whatever activity you were doing before being interrupted by the spontaneous occurrence of positive thoughts and feelings.

EXERCISE: Active Reflection

When first aware of a positive feeling, either pause for three to five minutes to engage in active reflection or record the experience in your positivity journal for later use. Follow these steps when practicing active reflection of positive intrusive thoughts and feelings:

Stop. Begin by finding a quiet place with minimal distractions. Sit in a comfortable chair and take slow, deep diaphragmatic breaths for thirty seconds. Focus your attention on the breath and allow your entire body to relax. Give yourself enough time to establish a state of calm, so you can focus on the pleasant feeling.

Think. Once you feel calm, recall the positive intrusive thought, image, or memory associated with the pleasant feeling. Be mindful of every aspect and detail of the positive image or memory you are recalling. If your attention drifts from the positive thought, gently bring it back to the intrusion.

Ponder. As you recall the positive intrusion, it is important to deeply reflect on it in order to maximize its effect on your emotional state. As you recall the positive intrusive thought, ask yourself these questions: *What does this thought say about me as a person—that is, my worth and value as a human being? Where did this thought come from? Why did I have this positive thought, image, or memory? What does the positive intrusive thought mean about my potential, my future, and quality of life? Does the thought reflect how others see me: how I am accepted and valued by others? What does the intrusive thought say about my potential for success, for making a meaningful contribution to society?*

At the end of your brief active-reflection session, use the following worksheet to record your experience with active reflection. In the first column, write the date. In the second column, write down the pleasant thoughts, images, or memories that you were recalling. Finally, in the third column, briefly note whether you could think deeply about the positive intrusive thought and whether this had a beneficial effect on your mood state.

Active-Reflection Worksheet

Date	Positive Thinking Targeted for Reflection	Outcome of Active Reflection
1.		
2.		
3.		
4.		
5.		

Completing the worksheet will help motivate you to practice active reflection. It's also a resource you can use to evaluate your progress. Are you getting better at increasing your sensitivity to the positive thoughts and feelings throughout your day? To continue practicing this skill, you can visit http://www.newharbinger.com/38426 to download other copies of the active-reflection worksheet.

Active reflection may seem awkward at first, so I recommend that you practice several times a day to improve your skill level. You can think of this skill as taking a five-minute break to dwell on positive mental interruptions. It will work best if you do active reflection when momentary happiness occurs. Soon-Yi tried to incorporate active-reflection breaks during the workday, but it proved difficult because of all the interruptions and work pressures. So she wrote down her uplifting moments in her positivity journal and then spent twenty minutes each night actively reflecting on her daily entries. You can boost the impact of positive intrusive thoughts and feelings by continuing to practice journaling and active reflection on a daily basis. Don't let your spontaneous positive thoughts and feelings become missed opportunities for momentary happiness!

Positive Reminiscence

One of the most powerful ways to encourage positive thoughts and feelings is by *cueing* them with an external or internal stimulus (a cue) that prompts specific thought content. For example, if you wanted to think about an enjoyable vacation you had last summer, you might look at vacation pictures. The photos would serve as a cue, prompting you to recall pleasant thoughts and feelings associated with the vacation. Music typically has a powerful cueing effect on our emotions. How often have you heard a familiar song from your youth and instantly felt a warm wave of nostalgia? But you don't have to leave cueing to chance.

Reminiscing about happy experiences from our past is one way to cue positive thoughts and feelings. Often this happens only when we're socializing with close friends or family. But there is no reason why we can't reminisce when alone. Researchers have found that intentionally recalling past positive events can increase our level of happiness (Chancellor, Layous, and Lyubomirsky 2015). If this is true, why not use positive memory recall as another strategy to boost your level of life satisfaction? Here are the steps for structuring a positive reminiscing session:

1. Create a list of cues that you can use to prime positive memories.

2. Schedule twenty to thirty minutes to do positive reminiscing in a quiet place where you can feel relaxed.

3. Choose a cue, such as vacation pictures, a favorite piece of music, a photo of a close friend, or something else, and spend several minutes looking at the photo, listening to the music: taking in the experience that the cue elicits.

4. Let positive memories come to your mind in response to the cue. Let yourself daydream, reflecting on the pleasant memory. Use your active-reflection skills to more deeply recall the memory and then record your experience on the worksheet in the next exercise.

This next exercise will help you enrich your positive reminiscing experiences.

EXERCISE: Cueing Positive Memory

Begin by writing down two to three specific cues in the related memory categories listed in the first column of the worksheet. These can be pictures, pieces of music, movies or videos, pieces of writing, a text, a Facebook post, or any object that serves as a cue for a positive memory. Choose one of these cues, and schedule a reminiscing session. Use the session to reflect deeply on the memory, and then write about your positive recollections in the second column. Rate your enjoyment level—how much you enjoyed or didn't enjoy reminiscing on a particular memory. Use a scale of -5 to 5, where -5 is very unenjoyable, 0 is neutral, and 5 is very enjoyable. This information will help you decide which cues work best for you. Continue to practice these memory sessions regularly until you sense they are having a positive effect on your mood state. Then practice this skill intermittently to reinforce positive feelings and overcome low mood.

List of Cues	Positive Recollections	Enjoyment Level (-5 to +5)
Pictures:		
Music:		
Movies/videos:		

Written material:		
Objects:		
People:		

Were you able to recall pleasant memories that were enjoyable and that generated momentary happiness? As you review your memory sessions, make note of the memories that were particularly enjoyable. These are the memories you'll want to recall when feeling blue and need a nudge in the positivity direction.

It's important to develop a variety of positive memories you can use to boost happiness. You can't expect your mood to improve by recalling the same thing over and over. You should have a mixture of pictures, music, videos, and objects that can prime a selection of cherished memories.

Soon-Yi didn't spend much time thinking about the past. She was very focused on the present and all the demands and pressures of her job. Even when she needed to relax, she never spent time reminiscing. So positive reminiscing was not a natural strategy for mood improvement. She had a difficult time at first coming up with a list of positive memory cues, but finally she was able to think of a couple of songs from her university days, some pictures of her last trip to Korea with a close friend, a T-shirt she got for completing her first 10-kilometer race, and some positive Facebook comments from her last posting.

147

After trying out these different cues, Soon-Yi found that music was most effective in priming positive memories of her youth, so she began using music as the cue for regular reminiscing sessions. Three to four times a week, Soon-Yi would set aside time in the evening to remember positive past experiences. With time she began to look forward to these sessions and noticed that her mood was more positive after she engaged in reminiscing. Her attitude was changing as well. She began to appreciate her life more and to realize she had much to be thankful for. Having a more positive perspective on herself and her life did much to raise Soon-Yi's general level of happiness and well-being. She began to feel more gratitude for the kindness that others had shown her.

Over time, cueing positive feelings can have a positive effect on your level of happiness and well-being even if it's not something that seems natural to you at first. So I encourage you to continue with this practice in addition to using active reflection and keeping a journal that emphasizes the positive moments in your life.

The Gratitude Effect

No doubt you've felt gratitude for an unexpected act of kindness, but have you ever considered the importance of this feeling? Gratitude is the recognition of receiving a benefit from someone's act of kindness (Lambert, Graham, and Fincham, 2009). We realize this kindness was given freely; we did nothing to earn it or deserve it. The expression of gratitude is also associated with increased positive emotion and well-being: a simple exercise like taking time once a week to list five or more things in your life for which you are thankful can significantly increase positive feelings (Emmons and McCullough 2003).

Soon-Yi learned she could increase her positive thoughts and feelings even more if she practiced thankfulness, by taking time to reflect on the life experiences recorded in her positivity journal and reminiscing sessions. Although she was stressed and unhappy most of the day, spending much of her time focused on daily hassles, Soon-Yi managed to schedule time each week to make a gratitude list and then communicate feelings of gratitude to her parents, close friends, and boyfriend. Together with other positivity skills, Soon-Yi discovered that authentic expressions of gratitude improved her general sense of well-being and life satisfaction.

Like Soon-Yi, feelings of gratitude might be in short supply in your daily life. If so, you are missing out on the positive effects of this powerful emotion. Rather than feel guilty about your lack of gratitude, why not do something about it by keeping a blessings diary, as described in the following exercise?

EXERCISE: The Blessings Diary

Periodically throughout the day, stop to consider whether some act of kindness has been extended toward you. It could be something significant or trivial, like a person letting you take a parking space rather than grabbing it for herself. In the second column of the blessings diary, make note of these acts of kindness or of complimentary comments that others have made. As well, take some time at the end of the day to consider your life more generally. As you think about your life in comparison to others, and what you are thankful for—such as good health, loving relationships, meaningful work, strong family ties, a faith community, freedom, and the list could go on—write these blessings in the third column. Over time, you can expand on this diary of blessings. If you need more space, you can visit http://www .newharbinger.com/38426 to download other copies of the blessings diary.

Date	Acts of Kindness or Complimentary Comments from Others	Blessings in My Life

After spending a couple of weeks on the blessings diary, take some time to review the diary. Are you surprised at the level of kindness shown toward you by others? As you read through the third column, are there more positive features to your life than you realized?

149

You can continue to use the blessings diary to help you practice the art of being grateful, and as you do this, you'll experience more positive emotion.

Happiness Reconsidered

Now that you've completed the work in this chapter, you can see that happiness is really an attitude, a state of mind. Feeling positive emotions like joy, interest, and amusement is only part of what it means to experience full life satisfaction. To reinforce the insights you've gained from this chapter, you may want to take a few minutes to do the following exercise.

EXERCISE: What Does Happiness Mean to You?

Do you remember exploring the question "What is happiness?" at the beginning of this chapter? After reading this chapter and working on the exercises, consider how you would answer these questions now.

1. What is happiness?

   _____

   _____

2. What would need to happen in your life to have more positive thoughts and feelings?

   _____

   _____

Do you notice any differences between your two sets of answers? Have you changed your view on happiness as a result of your work in this chapter? Possibly you never realized you had naturally occurring bursts of positive thoughts and feelings that could be used to enhance a greater sense of life satisfaction. Or, you've learned that you need to take time to reflect on the positive experiences in your daily life, or intentionally recall good memories, or practice the art of gratitude.

It's important not to miss the good in your life because of your focus on the stresses and burdens of everyday life. In all of this, it's hoped that you've discovered a new pathway to creating an emotional life less dominated by negativity and more attuned to positive thoughts and feelings.

Wrap-Up

Although people differ greatly in their life satisfaction, none of us needs to be stuck in a perpetual state of unhappiness. You can capitalize on your spontaneous moments of positive intrusive thoughts and feelings, using the strategies taught in this chapter:

- Know your baseline level of positivity to determine your general inclination for happiness or unhappiness.

- Begin making changes to increase daily positive thoughts and feelings. This starts by journaling momentary experiences of happiness to heighten your sensitivity to positive intrusive thoughts and feelings.

- Use active reflection to more deeply appreciate positive intrusive thoughts, daydreams, and memories, so you can maximize their influence on your daily mood.

- Schedule time to reminisce on pleasant past memories, which will prime positive mental intrusions.

- Regularly express gratitude for the gifts, benefits, and kindness you've received in this life.

As this workbook draws to a close, I hope you have found a greater sense of well-being and life satisfaction. If you are still feeling discouraged with your efforts to use the workbook strategies, the appendix can help you troubleshoot your mental-control issues. But whatever outcome you've achieved with this workbook, I encourage you to be persistent with your efforts and to not give up. As Confucius said, "It does not matter how slowly you go as long as you do not stop."

Acknowledgments

My understanding of emotional disorders has been informed by many wise and talented teachers, researchers, clinical supervisors, coinvestigators, and colleagues whom I have been privileged to know over my years as an academic and clinical psychologist. Several of these individuals are leading experts in cognitive behavioral treatment of psychological disorders, and their contribution to the ideas expressed in this workbook is substantial. For more than thirty years, I've had the honor of working with Dr. Aaron T. Beck, the father of cognitive therapy. He has inspired, challenged, and taught me much about mental health problems and their treatment. I count it an honor to call him a mentor, collaborator, and friend. I am also grateful to Professor S. Rachman and Dr. Padmal de Silva for their groundbreaking research on intrusive thoughts and for their mentorship during my graduate training.

There are a host of other clinical researchers whose innovative thinking, research, and creative therapy have made a significant contribution to the treatment of distressing, intrusive thoughts and feelings. This work spans various clinical domains, such as cognitive behavioral therapy, mindfulness, and acceptance and commitment therapy, as well as research into intrusive and repetitive thought, intentional mental control, the neural basis of unintended thought, and positive psychology. As such, this workbook is indebted to the work of Jon Abramowitz, Aaron T. Beck, Judith Beck, Brad Alford, Amparo Belloch, Mark Freeston, Randy Frost, Steven Hayes, Robert Leahy, S. Rachman, Adam Radomsky, Paul Salkovskis, Zindel Segal, Gail Steketee, John Teasdale, Daniel Wegner, Adrian Wells, and Mark Williams. I am also grateful to an especially talented group of graduate students, who collaborated with me on research into intrusive thinking and its control—Brendan Guyitt, Catherine Fraser, Mujgan Inozu, Christine Purdon, Gemma García-Soriano, and Adrienne Wang.

The ideas for *The Anxious Thoughts Workbook* have been percolating in my own mind for several years. However, this workbook would not be possible without the help and encouragement of others. I am grateful to my agent, Bob Diforio, who provided valuable expertise, advice, and unwavering support during preparation of this manuscript. He has been a valued advocate throughout this process, and I look forward to working together in the future. I want to thank Ryan Buresh, my acquisitions editor at New Harbinger, for the confidence he has shown in this project from its inception. Ryan, along with Clancy Drake, also provided valuable feedback on organization, style, and structure, which substantially improved the clarity, functionality, and message of the workbook.

I am also grateful for the opportunity to work with so many thoughtful and sensitive clients, who have taught me much about the real world of personal control. But most of all, I am indebted to my partner of four decades, Nancy Nason-Clark, a scholar and author in her own right, who has been a stalwart companion in life's journey. Nancy generously contributed to this workbook with her creativity, encouragement, and editorial wisdom. Without her involvement, this project would be greatly diminished.

Troubleshooting Your Mental-Control Issues

This appendix is for you if

1. You have come here right from the introduction because you would like to determine whether your negative thinking is the type of unwanted mental intrusion responsive to the self-directed skills presented in this workbook.

2. You have not made the progress you hoped for after working through this workbook.

3. You are a therapist interested in using this workbook with a client.

Learning mental-control skills is hard work. If you are not satisfied with your progress after completing *The Anxious Thoughts Workbook*, you may need to give yourself more time by practicing the skills taught in this workbook. But sometimes the type of thoughts you are experiencing won't respond well to self-help, and you will need a therapist's intervention. And sometimes self-help is not enough because you suffer from an underlying clinical condition, like major depression, OCD, or an anxiety disorder. This may or may not already be diagnosed.

Whether you have begun the work in this book or not, this appendix can help you determine whether you will benefit from the help of a skilled therapist or other resource in addition to the work you do here.

Are Your Mental Intrusions Wanted or Unwanted?

Ambivalence can undermine the effectiveness of self-directed mental control. This occurs when a negative intrusive thought, image, or memory has elements of being unwanted and wanted at the same time. For example, a negative thought pops into your mind, and you'd rather not have the thought (that is, it's unwanted), but then you end up dwelling on the negative thought as if you wanted to be thinking negatively. At other times, you'll hold on to your negative intrusions because you think they help you achieve a desired outcome. People can intentionally worry because they think it will help them solve a problem. When this happens, a distressing intrusive thought becomes wanted. To get a feel for *wanted intrusions*, consider the following examples.

- You're annoyed with your children and so you keep thinking about how you might have failed as a parent.

- A friend or coworker made a critical remark, and you keep thinking about it, wondering why she said such a thing.

- You're feeling depressed, and so you keep thinking about how you've failed in life.

- You've had an argument with your partner, and all you can think about is how unfair he's been treating you.

- You're anxious about a job interview, and you keep thinking about all the ways you make a poor impression on others.

It's important to remember that not all negative thinking is an unwanted mental intrusion. Once a negative thought, image, or memory becomes intentional, it will be more difficult to use this workbook's self-directed interventions. This is because you'll have a harder time reappraising the thought as insignificant, letting go of control, accepting the intrusion, and using more effective mental-control strategies. So it's important to know how much a negative thought is wanted, especially if you're finding it difficult to use the mental-control skills in this workbook.

Are you welcoming distressing thoughts, images, or memories into your mind? Samantha struggled terribly with this question when she had anxious intrusive thoughts about social situations. At first, the thought *I'm going to feel anxious* was an unwanted intrusion. However, sometimes she would dwell on the thought, intentionally trying to think about being anxious and how to calm herself down. On these occasions, what started as an unwanted intrusive thought became a wanted, intentional way of thinking. When your intrusive thoughts become wanted, a mental health professional trained in cognitive behaviorial therapy, mindfulness, and/or acceptance and commitment therapy could help you modify the mental-control interventions offered in this workbook to better address the increased personal investment in the distressing thought.

Are you wondering if you're more invested in your negative or anxious thinking than you first realized? The next exercise allows you to gauge the extent to which your distressing thoughts are wanted or unwanted.

EXERCISE: The Intrusion Wantedness Checklist

Begin this exercise by being aware of times over the next few days when you have a distressing intrusive thought, image, or memory. Each time this happens, place a checkmark (√) in the box next to any wantedness statements that apply to your experience of the thought on that occasion. Leave the box blank if the statement does not apply to your experience.

Wantedness of Intrusion	Occasions of Having Intrusion				
	1	2	3	4	5
1. *I intentionally tried to think about the thought, image, or memory.*					
2. *The thought was pleasant, pleasurable, or associated with a positive emotion.*					
3. *The intrusion helped me achieve a desired goal or outcome.*					
4. *The thought was highly acceptable to me.*					
5. *The thought was consistent with the type of person I am; that is, it was consistent with my character or how I see myself.*					

After completing the wantedness checklist over several days, review your entries and count the number of boxes you checked. If most of the statements were checked on several occasions, it's likely that a high degree of intentionality or wantedness is associated with the intrusive thought.

The strategies in this workbook are more difficult to use with wanted distressing thoughts, so you should consider whether therapist-assisted treatment would be more appropriate. Tell your therapist you seem to get caught up in the intrusion so that it becomes a wanted, highly intentional way of thinking. This will help your therapist design a treatment plan that considers your elevated personal investment in negative thinking.

Diagnosable Distress

Self-directed treatment is much more difficult if your anxiety, depression, obsessions, or another form of distress is highly intense and interferes in your ability to function. Mental health professionals use various guidelines to determine if a person's distress meets criteria for a diagnosable psychiatric disorder. If you are suffering from a diagnosable condition, then medication and more formal psychological treatment might be necessary. Of course, knowledge about mental control and its strategies can be useful with diagnosable conditions, but they may be more effective if incorporated in psychotherapy or systematic counseling. Although you may be trying hard to develop your mental-control skills, working on distressing intrusive thoughts on your own is not advisable when you are struggling with a diagnosable clinical condition.

Only a state-licensed mental health professional has the diagnostic knowledge and assessment tools to determine if your distress qualifies as a clinical disorder. The following checklist is provided to assist you in deciding whether you should obtain a mental health consultation.

EXERCISE: Detecting Diagnosable Distress

These statements represent different aspects of emotional distress. Place a checkmark (√) next to any statements that describe your experience with distress.

_____   *When I am upset, I tend to feel intense emotional distress.*

_____   *My distress can last for days or even weeks at a time.*

_____   *When I feel upset, it's very difficult to pull myself out of it.*

_____   *When I'm distressed, I can do very little; it greatly interferes in my ability to function.*

_____   *I can't sleep for several nights when feeling upset.*

_____   *I avoid many things to prevent feeling upset.*

_____   *When distressed, I become intensely critical of myself or others.*

_____   *I have a significant problem with anger.*

_____   *I have thoughts of hurting myself or others when I'm upset.*

_____   *I can isolate myself from friends and family for days when I'm upset.*

As you read through the checklist, did many of these statements describe your experience with personal distress? The more statements you checked, the greater the likelihood that your distress represents a clinical condition like major depression, an anxiety disorder, OCD, posttraumatic stress disorder, or the like. This is especially true if you've completed the workbook and found it hard to apply its interventions to your distressing intrusive thoughts and feelings. You can still use the mental-control strategies offered here, but you may find them more effective if they become part of a therapy or counseling program. The resources section provides a list of self-help books written for specific disorders as well as informative websites that can assist you in contacting qualified mental health professionals.

High-Risk Intrusive Thoughts

This workbook's strategies were not intended for use with *high-risk intrusive thoughts*, or distressing thoughts that are associated with a high risk of causing harm to self or others. If you have these types of thoughts, you should not attempt self-directed treatment but instead seek professional consultation as soon as possible. The following sections present various types of high-risk mental intrusions that require therapist-assisted treatment.

Suicidal Thoughts

When depressed, we can feel intense emotional pain. If you've been struggling with a serious depression, you may find the workbook helpful as a supplement to your therapist-delivered treatment. Medication, evidenced-based psychological treatment, or some combination of these can be highly effective for depression. However, this workbook's interventions are not designed to address suicidal thoughts associated with depression.

Suicidal thoughts are common with depression. When you are depressed, thoughts of death or of harming yourself can occur as unbidden intrusive thoughts, and these intrusions are high risk because people who are depressed often see their future as hopeless, they may believe that death is the only solution to life problems, and their wish to die may be stronger than their wish to live. Moreover, intrusive suicidal thoughts when someone is depressed can lead to suicidal plans and attempts. Therefore, if you or a loved one is depressed and experiencing suicidal thoughts, you should seek professional help immediately.

Sometimes thoughts can be mislabeled as "suicidal thoughts" when they do not really represent a desire to end your life. Not everyone who has thoughts of death is suicidal. For example, someone with anxiety may have the intrusive thought *What if I lose control and harm myself?* In that case, the person has a strong wish to live but is fearful of losing control. There is no hopelessness about the future, nor does the anxious person consider suicide a solution to life's problems. While the thought may be a very distressing one, it qualifies as a low-risk unwanted intrusion that can be treated with this workbook's strategies.

For example, for many years, a woman named Valeria struggled with anxiety and worry, but recently the anxiety took an unusual twist that took her by complete surprise. After hearing about the suicide of a young mother, Valeria started having frequent intrusive thoughts, such as *What drove this mother to suicide?* and *Could I just snap one day and kill myself, leaving my children alone and abandoned by their mother?* At first Valeria easily dismissed the thoughts from her mind, saying to herself *These are just crazy, stupid thoughts.* But the intrusions kept returning, and with them came a mounting sense of anxiety. It seemed like every unwanted occurrence of the intrusive thought was proof that she could lose control of her mind. Despite her anxiety, Valeria loved life. She cherished the time with her family and enjoyed the challenges of work. It was because of this engagement in life that she found her self-harm intrusions so threatening. Thus, Valeria's suicidal intrusions were low risk; they were truly unwanted mental intrusions and well suited for this workbook's strategies.

Violent and Aggressive Thoughts

We live in a violent society, with acts of aggression perpetuated daily at home, work, and in the community. Every year, millions of people are victims of violence, experiencing personal pain and suffering that can last a lifetime. All too often, violence and aggression happens in the home with devastating effects on parents, children, and partners. All forms of abuse whether physical, sexual, verbal or emotional have an adverse psychological effect on its victims. Thus, stopping violence must be of paramount importance in our society.

Anger, violence, and aggression often begin with an intrusive thought. The thought that you're being treated unfairly, manipulated, challenged, or threatened can trigger a process that culminates in violence. It can start with a benign intrusive thought like *That's not right*, but then it quickly escalates into *I've got to take charge, do something about this, to set matters right. I can't let this person take advantage of me.*

When spontaneous intrusive thoughts begin a cascading course of increasing anger and aggression toward others, it's important to first ensure the safety of others. This may involve reporting a violent family member to law enforcement. If you recognize violent and angry behavior in yourself, it's important to seek professional help before you cause harm to another person. Even if you're able to deescalate before becoming physically aggressive, your anger and verbal abuse will cause significant harm.

Accountability is critical in cases of anger and aggression, so trying to deal with your anger-related intrusions through self-help is inappropriate. A therapist is needed who can give expert guidance and provide monitoring tools, so you can work on your anger and aggression. Thoughts of fairness, justice, and power that lead to anger and aggression are high-risk intrusions that should not be left to self-directed mental-control intervention.

Delusional Thoughts

Sometimes intrusive thoughts are a profound misrepresentation of reality—so much so that the sufferer has difficulty knowing the difference between what is real and what is unreal. This problem became apparent for Marquis, who started having intrusive thoughts that he was unintentionally offending people, even strangers, simply by being present. If he walked into a grocery store, he immediately started thinking he had offended people who simply glanced at him. He became absolutely convinced that he had offended total strangers just by walking by them. So Marquis tried to avoid eye contact with people whenever he was in public. Of course, there was absolutely no evidence that people were offended, but this did not stop Marquis from believing he'd offended people. Marquis was confused, unable to discern reality from his distorted beliefs. His thinking was delusional and causing significant personal distress and inability to function. The good news is that Marquis began thinking more clearly about his intrusive thoughts once he saw a psychiatrist and started taking the correct medication. His perception of reality improved, and he was better able to evaluate his thoughts and beliefs.

If you find yourself firmly committed to an intrusive thought even though there is considerable evidence to the contrary, like Marquis, you may be suffering from delusional thinking. This workbook's mental-control strategies are not effective for this type of thinking. A psychiatric consultation is necessary in such cases. Often, medication can help clear up the confusion, misguided thinking, and distorted beliefs that characterize delusions. With the help of medication, you may be able to implement some of this workbook's control strategies. In the meantime, consider delusions another form of high-risk intrusive thinking that requires mental health intervention.

Dangerous and Misguided Fantasies

The imaginative power of the human brain is one of our greatest assets. We can create fantasies, daydreams, and imagined role-plays that are a great source of interest and pleasure. Of course, fantasies are significant in sexual arousal, and our great interest in movies and storytelling would not be possible without imagination. But sometimes our fantasies can become dark and destructive for ourselves, and if acted on, harmful to others. It is possible to spend too much time in fantasy, which then impedes our ability to interact in the real world. At other times, we may become overly preoccupied with a certain type of fantasy, especially sexual fantasy, which takes us to places that are self-destructive. Still other types of fantasies, such as sexual attraction to children or violent sexual encounters, are illegal and victimize others when encouraged.

What all these different types of fantasies have in common, especially the dark and destructive type, are three characteristics:

1. A strong association with pleasure

2. A high degree of intentionality or wantedness

3. A specific behavioral consequence

For example, an individual with sadistic sexual fantasies experiences pleasure from imagining violent sex with another person. He may actively seek out pornographic sites with violent sex and spend considerable time purposefully imagining these types of sexual encounters. It may eventually affect his behavior in the form of rough sex with partners.

Even if there is a certain degree of unwanted intrusiveness to your fantasies, this workbook's strategies are inappropriate for this type of thinking, and it is extremely difficult to change this type of thinking without professional help. Because pleasure is so strongly aroused by our fantasies, there is little interest in considering the intrusions insignificant. Therefore, self-directed mental control is inappropriate.

If your fantasies are tainted by dark, destructive, immoral, or even illegal elements, it is important that you seek out professional treatment before harm comes to you or others. These are high-risk intrusions that cannot be left to self-help intervention alone. Disclosure and accountability are important treatment elements for this type of cognitive activity.

Of course, sometimes people have unwanted intrusive thoughts or images that they consider repugnant and disgusting, such as an intrusive thought like *Am I sexually attracted to children?* In this case, the question is a horrifying, fearful thought. There is no sexual arousal associated with the intrusion, but instead there are feelings of anxiety, fear, and moral disgust. You may feel intense guilt and shame because the thought is such a violation of your moral code. If so, the intrusion is low risk, and this workbook's strategies are well suited for this type of problem. However, if the shame, guilt, or anxiety caused by these unwanted sexual intrusions is intense, you will need professional guidance to effectively use these mental-control skills.

Therapist-Assisted Mental Control

The Anxious Thoughts Workbook was written for people who want to work independently on their distressing thoughts and feelings. However, mental health professionals can also use this workbook as a client resource to boost the effectiveness of treatment. If your therapist has recommended this workbook, she may select certain exercises for you to emphasize and then incorporate this work into your therapy program. This workbook can also be used for therapy homework assignments as well as provide guidance and organization to your therapy.

At this point, you may be wondering if you should be relying on self-help alone or whether you should use the workbook with the assistance of a therapist. If you have not made the progress you hoped for after working through this workbook, the next exercise can help you decide whether you should seek out a therapist to assist you with these interventions.

EXERCISE: A Help-Seeking Guide

Place a checkmark (√) beside each statement that applies to your experience with *The Anxious Thoughts Workbook*.

_____   *For several weeks, I've been trying to use the mental-control strategies in chapter 7, but my anxiety, depression, obsessions, guilt, or other distressing emotion remains unchanged.*

_____   *My distressing thoughts are more like the high-risk intrusive thoughts discussed in this appendix.*

_____   *Despite working through the exercises in chapters 1 and 4, I remain highly invested in my intrusive thoughts. That is, I still believe these negative thoughts are significant, meaningful ideas that must be suppressed.*

_____   *I remain convinced that I must try harder to control my distressing mental intrusions.*

_____   *I am struggling with self-acceptance and have little tolerance for my distressing intrusive thoughts.*

_____   *I keep getting drawn back into one of the weak or ineffective mental-control strategies discussed in chapter 5.*

_____   *My negative thoughts, ideas, and memories are becoming more frequent and upsetting despite my best efforts to use the workbook strategies.*

How many of the statements did you endorse? Even if you checked only one statement, you might consider using the workbook as a supplement to therapy.

It's possible you'll get more from the workbook if it's incorporated into your therapy. The advantage of using the workbook in this way is that a therapist can tailor the mental-control interventions so they target unique aspects of your distressing thoughts and feelings. Making fundamental changes in how we think and feel is the hardest work anyone can undertake. Sometimes it is possible to do this work alone, but other times professional help is needed.

What's important is that you give yourself the best possible opportunity to recover from your emotional distress. Whether you have tried this workbook's interventions with only limited success or you are unsure about learning these new skills on your own, consider whether you might get more benefit by working with a mental health professional.

Wrap-Up

After reading this appendix, you might be wondering if you're getting the most from *The Anxious Thoughts Workbook*. In the end, the best test is how you feel. Have you been able to use the workbook interventions to reduce your emotional distress? If not, and you would like to obtain greater distress relief, consider troubleshooting your mental-control efforts. Several problems were highlighted in this appendix that may be undermining your efforts to change.

- Consider whether your distressing thoughts are more wanted than unwanted. You'll find the workbook strategies more difficult to use when your intrusive thoughts are intentional, highly accepted forms of thought.

- Consider whether you might be struggling with a clinical disorder like major depression, an anxiety disorder, or OCD. If so, you can expect self-directed treatment to be less successful than working with a mental health professional.

- If your distressing thoughts are high-risk intrusions that have serious negative consequences to yourself or others, then taking a self-help approach to mental control is not appropriate. Thoughts of suicidal intent, anger and aggression, confusion of reality, and misdirected fantasies are best treated by a mental health professional.

- Consider whether you might get more out of this workbook by using it as a client resource tool during a course of psychotherapy.

If this workbook's strategies have not led to significant improvement in your mental and emotional state, I hope the information, recommendations, and exercises provided in this appendix have been helpful in your troubleshooting efforts. I also encourage you to review the resources section to see if any of these additional self-help materials might be especially appropriate for your type of personal distress. Many of these resources are more focused and disorder-specific than this workbook, and they tackle negative thoughts and feelings from a different perspective.

Resources

Selected Websites: Information on Evidence-Based Psychological Treatments

These websites provide information on the nature of various psychological problems as well as treatment information for anxiety, depression, obsessions, and other emotional conditions. Many provide online tools that can help you find certified practitioners in your region.

Academy of Cognitive Therapy, Philadelphia; http://www.academyofct.org

Association for Behavioral and Cognitive Therapies (ABCT), New York; http://www.abct.org

Association for Contextual Behavioral Science, Jenison, MI; http://www.contextualscience .org

Beck Institute for Cognitive Behavior Therapy, Bala Cynwyd, PA; http://www.beckinstitute .org

Center for Mindfulness in Medicine, Health Care, and Society, University of Massachusetts Medical School; http://www.umassmed.edu/cfm

Canadian Association of Cognitive Behaviour Therapies (CACBT), Quebec City; http://www .cacbt.ca

Selected Websites: Information on Mental Health and Its Treatment

These websites provide a wide range of information on mental health issues, including diverse treatment approaches to mental health problems.

American Psychological Association (APA), Washington, DC; http://www.apa.org

Anxiety and Depression Association of America (ADAA), Silver Spring, MD; http://www.adaa.org

Canadian Psychological Association (CPA), Ottawa; http://www.cpa.ca

National Institute of Mental Health (NIMH), Bethesda, MD; http://www.nimh.nih.gov

Recommended Reading

The Anger Management Workbook: Use the STOP Method to Replace Destructive Responses with Constructive Behavior, by W. R. Nay. 2014. New York: Guilford Press.

The Anxiety and Worry Workbook: The Cognitive Behavioral Solution, by D. A. Clark and A. T. Beck. 2012. New York: Guilford Press.

Anxiety Free: Unravel Your Fears Before They Unravel You, by R. L. Leahy. 2009. Carlsbad, CA: Hay House.

Beat the Blues Before They Beat You: How to Overcome Depression, by R. L. Leahy. 2010. Carlsbad, CA: Hay House.

The Dialectical Behavior Therapy Skills Workbook, by M. McKay, J. C. Wood, and J. Brantley. 2007. Oakland, CA: New Harbinger Publications.

Getting over OCD: A 10-Step Workbook for Taking Back Your Life, by J. S. Abramowitz. 2009. New York: Guilford Press.

Get Out of Your Mind and into Your Life: The New Acceptance and Commitment Therapy, by S. C. Hayes. 2005. Oakland, CA: New Harbinger Publications.

Mind over Mood: Change How You Feel by Changing the Way You Think, 2nd ed., by D. Greenberger and C. A. Padesky. 2016. New York: Guilford Press.

The Mindfulness and Acceptance Workbook for Anxiety, 2nd ed., by J. P. Forsyth and G. H. Eifert. 2016. Oakland, CA: New Harbinger Publications.

The Mindfulness and Acceptance Workbook for Depression, by K. D. Strosahl and P. J. Robinson. 2008. Oakland, CA: New Harbinger Publications.

The Mindful Way Workbook: An 8-Week Program to Free Yourself from Depression and Emotional Distress, by J. Teasdale, M. Williams, and Z. Segal. 2014. New York: Guilford Press.

The Mood Repair Toolkit: Proven Strategies to Prevent the Blues from Turning into Depression, by D. A. Clark. 2014. New York: Guilford Press.

Overcoming Obsessive Thoughts: How to Gain Control of Your OCD, by C. Purdon and D. A. Clark. 2005. Oakland, CA: New Harbinger Publications.

Overcoming Unwanted Intrusive Thoughts, by S.M. Winston and M.N. Seif. 2017. Oakland, CA: New Harbinger Publications.

The Practicing Happiness Workbook, by R. Baer. 2014. Oakland, CA: New Harbinger Publications.

The Worry Cure: Seven Steps to Stop Worry from Stopping You, by R. L. Leahy. 2005. New York: Three Rivers Press.

Worry Less, Live More: The Mindful Way Through Anxiety Workbook, by S. M. Orsillo and L. Roemer. 2016. New York: Guilford Press.

References

American Psychiatric Association. 2013. *Diagnostic And Statistical Manual Of Mental Disorders, Fifth Edition (DSM-V)*. 5th ed. Washington, DC: American Psychiatric Association.

Baars, B. J. 2010. "Spontaneous Repetitive Thoughts Can Be Adaptive: Postscript on 'Mind Wandering.'" *Psychological Bulletin* 136 (2): 208–10.

Baer, R. 2014. *The Practicing Happiness Workbook*. Oakland, CA: New Harbinger Publications.

Barahmand, U. 2009. "Meta-Cognitive Profiles in Anxiety Disorders." *Psychiatry Research* 169 (3): 240–43.

Bauer, I. M., and R. F. Baumeister. 2011. "Self-Regulatory Strength." In *Handbook of Self-Regulation: Research, Theory, and Application*, 2nd ed., edited K. D. Vohs and R. F. Baumeister. New York: Guilford Press.

Beck, A. T. 1967. *Depression: Causes and Treatment*. Philadelphia: University of Pennsylvania Press.

Beck, A. T., A. J. Rush, B. F. Shaw, and G. Emery. 1979. *Cognitive Therapy of Depression*. New York: Guilford Press.

Beck, J. S. 2011. *Cognitive Behavior Therapy: Basics and Beyond*. 2nd ed. New York: Guilford Press.

Bjornsson, A. S., and K. A. Phillips. 2014. "Do Obsessions and Compulsions Play a Role in Social Anxiety Disorder?" *Harvard Review of Psychiatry* 22 (1): 55–58.

Borkovec, T. D., L. Wilkinson, R. Folensbee, and C. Lerman. 1983. "Stimulus Control Applications to the Treatment of Worry." *Behaviour Research and Therapy* 21 (3): 247–51.

Cartwright-Hatton, S., and A. Wells. 1997. "Beliefs About Worry and Intrusions: The Meta-Cognitions Questionnaires and Its Correlates." *Journal of Anxiety Disorders* 11 (3): 279–96.

Chancellor, J., K. Layous, and S. Lyubomirsky. 2015. "Recalling Positive Events at Work Makes Employees Feel Happier, Move More, But Interact Less: A 6-Week Randomized Controlled Intervention at a Japanese Workplace." *Journal of Happiness Studies* 16 (4): 871–87.

Christoff, K. 2012. "Undirected Thought: Neural Determinants and Correlates." *Brain Research* 1428: 51–59.

Clark, D. A. 2004. *Cognitive Behavioral Therapy for OCD.* New York: Guilford Press.

Clark, D.A., and A. T. Beck. 2012. *The Anxiety and Worry Workbook: The Cognitive Behavioral Solution.* New York: Guilford Press.

Clark, D. A., A. T. Beck, and B. Alford. 1999. *Scientific Foundations of Cognitive Theory and Therapy of Depression.* New York: John Wiley and Sons.

Clark, D. A., C. Purdon, and E. S. Byers. 2000. "Appraisal and Control of Sexual and Non-Sexual Intrusive Thoughts in University Students." *Behaviour Research and Therapy* 38: 439–455.

Clark, D. A., and S. Rhyno. 2005. "Unwanted Intrusive Thoughts in Nonclinical Individuals: Implications for Clinical Disorders." In *Intrusive Thoughts in Clinical Disorders: Theory, Research and Treatment,* edited by David A. Clark. New York: Guilford Press.

Conway, M., A. Howell, and C. Giannopoulas. 1991. "Dysphoria and Thought Suppression." *Cognitive Therapy and Research* 15 (2): 153–66.

Cummins, R. A., and H. Nistico. 2002. "Maintaining Life Satisfaction: The Role of Positive Cognitive Bias." *Journal of Happiness Studies* 3 (1): 37–69.

Diener, E. 2000. "Subjective Well-Being: The Science of Happiness and a Proposal for a National Index." *The American Psychologist* 55 (1): 34–43.

Diener, E., R. E. Lucas, and C. N. Scollon. 2006. "Beyond the Hedonic Treadmill: Revising the Adaptation Theory of Well-Being." *The American Psychologist* 61 (4): 305–14.

Diener, E., E. M. Suh, R. E. Lucas, and H. L. Smith. 1999. "Subjective Well-Being: Three Decades of Progress." *Psychological Bulletin* 125 (2): 276–302.

Dixon, M. L., K. C. Fox, and K. Christoff. 2014. "A Framework for Understanding the Relationship Between Externally and Internally Directed Cognition." *Neuropsychologia* 62: 321–30.

Edwards, S., and M. Dickerson. 1987. "On the Similarity of Positive and Negative Intrusions." *Behaviour Research and Therapy* 25 (3): 207–11.

Emmons, R. A., and M. E. McCullough. 2003. "Counting Blessings Versus Burdens: An Experimental Investigation of Gratitude and Subjective Well-Being in Daily life." *Journal of Personality and Social Psychology* 84 (2): 377–89.

Fava, G. A., and L. Mangelli. 2001. "Assessment of Subclinical Symptoms and Psychological Well-Being in Depression." *European Archives of Clinical Neuroscience* 251 (Suppl. 2): 1147–1152.

Fredrickson, B. L., and M. F. Losada. 2005. "Positive Affect and the Complex Dynamics of Human Flourishing." *The American Psychologist* 60 (7): 678–86.

Freeston, M., R. Ladouceur, M. Provencher, and F. Blais. 1995. "Strategies Used with Intrusive Thoughts: Context, Appraisal, Mood, and Efficacy." *Journal of Anxiety Disorders* 9 (3): 201–15.

Greenberger, D., and C. A. Padesky. 2016. *Mind over Mood: Change How You Feel by Changing the Way You Think.* 2nd ed. New York: Guilford Press.

Halvorsen, M., R. Hagen, O. Hjemdal, M. Eriksen, Å Sørli, K. Waterloo, M. Eisemann, and C. Wang. 2015. "Metacognitions and Thought Control Strategies in Unipolar Major Depression: A Comparison of Currently Depressed, Previously Depressed, and Never-Depressed Individuals." *Cognitive Therapy and Research* 39 (1): 31–40.

Hayes, S. C., K. D. Strosahl, and K. G. Wilson. 2011. *Acceptance and Commitment Therapy: The Process and Practice of Mindful Change.* 2nd ed. New York: Guilford Press.

Janeck, A. S., J. E. Calamari, B. C. Riemann, and S. K. Heffelfinger. 2003. "Too Much Thinking About Thinking?: Metacognitive Differences in Obsessive-Compulsive Disorder." *Journal of Anxiety Disorders* 17 (2): 181–95.

Kessler, R. C., W. T. Chiu, O. Demler, and E. E. Walters. 2005. "Prevalence, Severity, and Comorbidity of Twelve-Month DSM-IV Disorders in the National Comorbidity Survey Replication (NCS-R)." *Archives of General Psychiatry* 62 (6): 617–27.

Killingsworth, M. A., and D. T. Gilbert. 2010. "A Wandering Mind Is an Unhappy Mind." *Science* 330 (6006): 932.

Koole, S. L., and A. van Knippenberg. 2007. "Controlling Your Mind Without Ironic Consequences: Self-Affirmation Eliminates Rebound Effects After Thought Suppression." *Journal of Experimental Social Psychology* 43 (4): 671–77.

Lambert, N. M., S. M. Graham, and F. D. Fincham. 2009. "A Prototype Analysis of Gratitude: Varieties of Gratitude Experiences." *Personality and Social Psychology Bulletin* 35 (9): 1193–207.

Leahy, R. L., D. Tirch, and L. A. Napolitano. 2011. *Emotion Regulation in Psychotherapy: A Practitioner's Guide.* New York: Guilford Press.

Lyubomirsky, S., L. King, and E. Diener. 2005. "The Benefits of Frequent Positive Affect: Does Happiness Lead to Success?" *Psychological Bulletin* 131 (6): 803–55.

Mischel, W. 2014. *The Marshmallow Test: Why Self-Control Is the Engine of Success*. New York: Little Brown and Company.

Munoz, E., M. J. Sliwinski, J. M. Smyth, D. M. Almeida, and H. King. 2013. "Intrusive Thoughts Mediate the Association Between Neuroticism and Cognitive Performance." *Personality and Individual Differences* 55 (8): 898–903.

Najmi, S., B. C. Riemann, and D. M .Wegner,. 2009. "Managing Unwanted Intrusive Thoughts in Obsessive-Compulsive Disorder: Relative Effectiveness of Suppression, Focused Distraction, and Acceptance." *Behaviour Research and Therapy* 47 (6): 494–503.

Purdon, C., and D. A. Clark. 1994. "Obsessive Intrusive Thoughts in Nonclinical Subjects: Part II. Cognitive Appraisal, Emotional Response and Thought Control Strategies." *Behaviour Research and Therapy* 32 (4): 403–10.

Rachman, S. 1981. "Part I. Unwanted Intrusive Cognitions." *Advances in Behaviour Research and Therapy* 3 (3): 89–99.

———. 2003. *The Treatment of Obsessions*. Oxford: Oxford University Press.

Radomsky, A. S., G. M. Alcolado, J. S. Abramowitz, P. Alonso, A. Belloch, M. Bouvard, D. A. Clark, et al. 2014. "Part 1—You Can Run But You Can't Hide: Intrusive Thoughts on Six Continents." *Journal of Obsessive-Compulsive and Related Disorders* 3 (3): 269–79.

Rassin, E. 2005. *Thought Suppression*. Amsterdam: Elsevier.

Roemer, L., and T. D. Borkovec. 1993. "Worry: Unwanted Cognitive Activity That Controls Unwanted Somatic Experience." In *Handbook of Mental Control*, edited by D. M. Wegner and J. W. Pennebaker. Upper Saddle River, NJ: Prentice Hall.

Roemer, L., and S. M. Orsillo. 2009. *Mindfulness and Acceptance-Based Behavioral Therapies in Practice*. New York: Guilford Press.

Salkovskis, P. M., and O. Kobori. 2015. "Reassuringly Calm? Self-Reported Patterns of Responses to Reassurance Seeking in Obsessive Compulsive Disorder." *Journal of Behavior Therapy and Experimental Psychiatry* 49 (Part B): 203–8.

Steele, C. M. 1988. "The Psychology of Self-Affirmation: Sustaining the Integrity of the Self." In *Advances in Experimental Social Psychology*, vol. 21, edited by L. Berkowitz. San Diego, CA: Academic Press.

Teasdale, J., M. Williams, and Z. Segal. 2014. *The Mindful Way Workbook: An 8-Week Program to Free Yourself from Depression and Emotional Distress*. New York: Guilford Press.

Vohs, K. D., and R. F. Baumeister, eds. 2011. *Handbook of Self-Regulation: Research, Theory, and Applications*. 2nd ed. New York: Guilford Press.

Wagner, D. D., and T. F. Heatherton. 2011. "Giving in to Temptation: The Emerging Cognitive Neuroscience of Self-Regulatory Failure." In *Handbook of Self-Regulation: Research, Theory, and Application*, 2nd ed., edited by K. D. Vohs and R. F. Baumeister. New York: Guilford Press.

Wegner, D. M. 1994a. "Ironic Processes of Mental Control." *Psychological Review* 101 (1): 34–52.

———. 1994b. *White Bears and Other Unwanted Thoughts: Suppression, Obsession, and the Psychology Mental Control*. New York: Guilford Press.

———. 2011. "Setting Free the Bears: Escape from Thought Suppression." *The American Psychologist* 66 (8): 671–80.

Wegner, D. M., and J. W. Pennebaker, eds. 1993. *Handbook of Mental Control*. Englewood Cliffs, NJ: Prentice-Hall.

Wiggins, G. A., and J. Bhattacharya. 2014. "Mind the Gap: An Attempt to Bridge Computational and Neuroscientific Approaches to Study Creativity." *Frontiers in Human Neuroscience* 8: 540. http://dx.doi.org/10.3389/fnhum.2014.00540.

David A. Clark, PhD, is a practicing clinical psychologist and professor emeritus at the University of New Brunswick, Canada. He is author or coauthor of numerous scientific articles and nine books on depression, anxiety, and obsessive-compulsive disorder (OCD), including *The Mood Repair Toolkit*, *The Anxiety and Worry Workbook* (with Aaron T. Beck), and *Overcoming Obsessive Thoughts* (with Christine Purdon). A founding fellow and trainer consultant with the Academy of Cognitive Therapy, and fellow of the Canadian Psychological Association, Clark resides in Canada.

Foreword writer **Judith Beck, PhD**, is director of the Beck Institute for Cognitive Therapy, clinical associate professor of psychology in psychiatry at the University of Pennsylvania, and past president of the Academy of Cognitive Therapy. The daughter of influential founder of cognitive therapy, Aaron T. Beck, Beck resides in Bala Cynwyd, PA. She is author of *The Beck Diet Solution*.

MORE BOOKS *from*
NEW HARBINGER PUBLICATIONS

COPING WITH ANXIETY,
SECOND EDITION
Ten Simple Ways to Relieve Anxiety,
Fear & Worry
978-1626253858 / US $15.95

THE RELAXATION & STRESS
REDUCTION WORKBOOK,
SIXTH EDITION
978-1572245495 / US $24.95

THE WORRY TRICK
How Your Brain Tricks You
into Expecting the Worst & What
You Can Do About It
978-1626253186 / US $16.95

END THE
INSOMNIA STRUGGLE
A Step-by-Step Guide to Help You
Get to Sleep & Stay Asleep
978-1626253438 / US $24.95

NATURAL RELIEF
FOR ANXIETY
Complementary Strategies for Easing
Fear, Panic & Worry
978-1572243729 / US $18.95

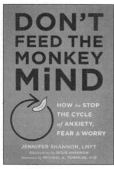

DON'T FEED THE
MONKEY MIND
How to Stop the Cycle of
Anxiety, Fear, & Worry
978-1626255067 / US $16.95

newharbingerpublications
1-800-748-6273 / newharbinger.com

(VISA, MC, AMEX / prices subject to change without notice)

Follow Us 🇫 🐦 📷 📌

ARE YOU SEEKING A CBT THERAPIST?

The Association for Behavioral & Cognitive Therapies (ABCT) Find-a-Therapist service offers
a list of therapists schooled in CBT techniques. Therapists listed are licensed professionals who
have met the membership requirements of ABCT & who have chosen to appear in the directory.
Please visit www.abct.org & click on *Find a Therapist.*

Sign up for our Book Alerts at **newharbinger.com/bookalerts**

Register your **new harbinger** titles for additional benefits!

When you register your **new harbinger** title—purchased in any format, from any source—you get access to benefits like the following:

- Downloadable accessories like printable worksheets and extra content

- Instructional videos and audio files

- Information about updates, corrections, and new editions

Not every title has accessories, but we're adding new material all the time.

Access free accessories in 3 easy steps:

1. Sign in at NewHarbinger.com (or **register** to create an account).

2. Click on **register a book**. Search for your title and click the **register** button when it appears.

3. Click on the **book cover or title** to go to its details page. Click on **accessories** to view and access files.

That's all there is to it!

If you need help, visit:

NewHarbinger.com/accessories

new harbinger
CELEBRATING
40 YEARS